THE HOPEFUL ACTIVIST

THE HOPEFUL ACTIVIST

Discovering the vital change
you were made to bring

Rich Gower and Rachel Walker

Foreword by Ruth Valerio

First published in Great Britain in 2024

SPCK
SPCK Group
Studio 101
The Record Hall
16–16A Baldwin's Gardens
London EC1N 7RJ

www.spck.org.uk

British Library Cataloguing-in-Publication Data
A catalogue record for this book is available from the British Library

ISBN 978-0-281-08824-9
eBook ISBN 978-0-281-08825-6

1 3 5 7 9 10 8 6 4 2

Typeset by Fakenham Prepress Solutions, Fakenham, Norfolk NR21 8NL
First printed in Great Britain by

eBook by Fakenham Prepress Solutions, Fakenham, Norfolk NR21 8NL

Produced on paper from sustainable forests

Contents

Contents

Foreword

I'm writing this having just come back from a food waste initiative called UKHarvest. It's run by a local charity that collects surplus food from supermarkets, restaurants and so on, and delivers it to hubs around the area, one of which is my nearby parish church, which opens its hall for the hub once a fortnight. Anyone can go down on that morning, make a small donation and fill up a bag with food. Refreshments are served and folks sit around tables chatting. It's a brilliant initiative, particularly for people struggling financially. It also highlights our terrible, broken food system and the absolute travesty of vast amounts of good-quality food going to waste every day.

My neighbour is a volunteer and I go down with her whenever I can. I love seeing the church partnering with something so positive, and it's a really good way to sit and have a chat with people from the estate I live on, which is near the church (and the food is an added bonus!). I've lived on this council housing estate for nearly my whole adult life, having moved there initially as part of a church plant. The church plant sadly didn't continue for very long, but my life on the estate did, and I've been very involved there, setting up and co-chairing the community association for twelve years. We became a great little team of local residents and, together, worked hard to transform the estate from one that had all the crime-ridden hallmarks of an economically deprived social housing development into an attractive place that people enjoy living in. Crime rates have dropped significantly and people take pride in the area.

It was incredibly hard work, of course. There was many an evening when I thought I'd really rather stay in and watch TV than go out to a community meeting or walk around the streets putting leaflets through doors. We faced resistance from local residents who didn't believe anything good could happen on the estate, and opposition from the police and local authorities who didn't want to have to engage with the antisocial issues we were facing. And we were totally ignorant! We didn't know the first thing about community action or fundraising or how the power structures worked.

We learned – as much through the things we did wrong as through our successes – but I wish I had been able to read this book back then. It would have been enormously helpful.

Activism is in my heart. Whether it's working to see transformation in my local community; helping people escape to a new life from the brothels and drug dens of an Asian megacity; sitting on the streets with people who are homeless; or campaigning against climate change and environmental destruction, I believe that God has called me to 'spend [myself] on behalf of the hungry and satisfy the needs of the oppressed'.[1]

And not only me. All of us are called to find our place in God's big story of redemption and transformation and to live lives that, in our own individual ways, work towards the future where there will be no more suffering or tears;

where trees flourish and heal, and the waters run clear and bring life.[2]

But how do we discover what that looks like for each one of us? How do we live out our calling well, and how do we keep going and not burn out as we do so? It is these and other questions that *The Hopeful Activist* explores so helpfully. If you're just starting to sense God's stirring, then this book is for you and will be an invaluable guide that accompanies you on your journey. If you've been walking this path for years, *The Hopeful Activist* will re-inspire you, remind you why you're doing what you're doing, and give you fresh tools as you work for justice and transformation.

Wherever we are and whatever we're doing, may we work together to see God's kingdom come and his will be done on this earth *now* as it is in heaven.

Ruth Valerio

Introduction

There are a few different ways to read this book. Wherever you are in your activism journey, we'd recommend starting with chapter 1, which lays the foundation for everything else that follows.

After going through the first chapter, though, you might want to jump straight to a chapter that addresses a particular challenge you are facing right now. So, if you feel as if your theology of activism needs a refresh, check out chapter 2. If you're trying to work out what to do with your life (or even with just a couple of spare hours a week!) then there's advice for you in chapters 3 and 4. If you are working on a project or a campaign and need some practical wisdom, then you might want to head for chapter 5, followed by chapter 6 or chapter 7. If you're trying to build a team, or are finding team dynamics challenging, that's covered in chapter 8. And if you're reading this and feeling on the edge of burnout, chapter 9 is written for you.

You can of course read the book in the traditional way (it will probably flow best like this). And you could also do so as a group; many of the basic ideas in the book have been road-tested through our Praxis Labs courses, where we've found that group discussions can be really helpful in deepening our reflections and moving us towards action. There are reflection questions at the end of each chapter that can be used for solo reflection or group discussion.

However you read this book, our hope and prayer is that it both helps you find your unique role in God's story and helps you play that role effectively. Happy reading!

1

Living the questions

If you have picked up this book and are reading these words, the likelihood is that you are, in some way, an activist (even if you don't know it yet). You see problems in the world, situations happening that are *just not right*, and you want to be a part of addressing them.

Perhaps, although you would call yourself a doer, you don't know where to start. Or perhaps you have been busy 'doing', and you now want to step back and think through where this drive comes from. Maybe you're a Christian like us, but your faith background hasn't given you much of a framework for engaging in activism, so you want to figure out how justice can factor into your walk with God.

The purpose of this guide is to help you find your unique role in God's story, particularly in relation to justice. It's informed by interviews with more than a hundred activists, theologians and pioneers, and you'll see a few of them pop up to offer their wisdom and advice over the next ten chapters. We're part of the team behind a podcast called *The Hopeful Activists*, and all our learning from that is folded into these pages. We've also had the immense privilege of going back and interviewing several of the activists and theologians who have inspired us the most, specifically for this book.

The aim of this first chapter is to lay the foundations for the rest of the book. We're big fans of a good question well crafted, and we think Jesus, as we see him in the Gospels, was too, so we've called it 'Living the questions',[1] a phrase borrowed from the Northumbria Community.[2] Each chapter will feature at least one question for reflection, and the purpose of these isn't to produce a single, simple answer. It's to prompt a process of exploration – to 'live the questions', if you like – in our thinking and our action. Here's one to start you off: **What can you do today that will last into eternity?**

If you like, grab a pencil, and scribble some thoughts in the margin here, or in a journal.

***

As activists, it's tempting to want to get on and do stuff, to fix problems, to change the world! But our answers to questions like the one above should lay the foundation for our action. Our days are spent in relationship with God, the world and those around us. These relationships are always growing, developing and changing, and asking good questions of ourselves helps to stimulate this growth.

A similarly foundational question for us to get to grips with is 'Why?' You may have heard the phrase 'Know your why' before; it's often a favourite of motivational speakers. And there's a reason it's motivational! If we know and have a deep understanding of our answer to the question 'Why am I doing this?', it helps us to go the distance when things are hard. (We'll talk about this a little more in chapter 4.)

'Living the questions' can be a bit like learning from Jesus' parables. When we read a parable today, we often think of it as an illustration for an idea, because that's how we use stories in our culture. You may have experienced this in practice at a church service during the sermon: a preacher makes three points and, after each one, provides an anecdote to illustrate it, developing the point in a humorous or emotive way. (It's often an effective technique. I (Rich) can still remember an anecdote from more than a decade ago about a toddler sassily refusing banana-flavoured medicine, but I'm more hazy about the point that was being made!)

However, that's not the way that Jesus, in his ancient Middle Eastern culture, used stories. Theologian Kenneth Bailey, in his book *Jesus through Middle Eastern Eyes*, put it this way:

> A parable is not a delivery system for an idea, but a house in which the reader is invited to take up residence. The reader is invited to look at the world through the windows of that residence. The reader is encouraged to examine the human predicament through the worldview created by the parable.[3]

A parable is not an anecdote; it is something you live in. It creates meaning. It gets behind your defences. This understanding has prompted us to engage with Jesus' parables more thoughtfully, and hopefully some of the prompts in this book will serve in the same way, providing questions that we can live our way into.

So, let's look at a parable that will probably be very familiar: the Parable of the Good Samaritan in Luke chapter 10. We've used the *Message* version. As you read it, why not try to imagine yourself in the crowd around Jesus, hearing this for the first time? Put yourself in the scene. It's hot, it's dusty, there's a gentle breeze . . .

Just then a religion scholar stood up with a question to test Jesus. 'Teacher, what do I need to do to get eternal life?'

He answered, 'What's written in God's Law? How do you interpret it?'

He said, 'That you love the Lord your God with all your passion and prayer and muscle and intelligence – and that you love your neighbor as well as you do yourself.'

'Good answer!' said Jesus. 'Do it and you'll live.'

Looking for a loophole, he asked, 'And just how would you define "neighbor"?'

Jesus answered by telling a story. 'There was once a man traveling from Jerusalem to Jericho. On the way he was attacked by robbers. They took his clothes, beat him up, and went off leaving him half-dead. Luckily, a priest was on his way down the same road, but when he saw him he angled across to the other side. Then a Levite religious man showed up; he also avoided the injured man.

'A Samaritan traveling the road came on him. When he saw the man's condition, his heart went out to him. He gave him first aid, disinfecting and bandaging his wounds. Then he lifted him onto his donkey, led him to an inn, and made him comfortable. In the morning he took out two silver coins and gave them to the innkeeper, saying, "Take good care of him. If it costs any more, put it on my bill – I'll pay you on my way back."

'What do you think? Which of the three became a neighbor to the man attacked by robbers?'

'The one who treated him kindly,' the religion scholar responded.

Jesus said, 'Go and do the same.'[4]

Were you able to immerse yourself in the story? Why not give it another read-through? There is so much in the parable – it's certainly a house you could live in for a while.

There are two observations we can start with.

Observation 1

Jesus doesn't answer the scholar's questions with simple answers. First, he effectively asks the man, 'What do you think?' Second, he tells a story which finishes with a question. Jesus likes stories and questions!

His response is very different from how we might respond in British (or church) culture today. If we were asked a question such as 'What must I do to get eternal life?', we might try to come up with a straightforward response outlining how to behave and what to do and pray; maybe we'd even supply a handy four-step guide. Alternatively, in some circles, we might go the opposite way and embrace the theoretical, creating layer upon layer of complexity in a deep theological response. Neither of these is necessarily wrong – practical guidance and deep theology are helpful – but in this instance, they're not what Jesus gives as a response.

What the religious teacher seems to want is a formula to live by, a list of people he must care for and be kind to. Jesus doesn't provide it, giving him a *story* to live by instead. This account is so familiar to us that we can miss this crucial point, particularly as it's not how we operate nowadays! Living by this story, this parable, invites us to ask deep questions about how we view and value others, and how we view ourselves.

Living the questions helps us to be honest with God, with ourselves and with others, allowing us to navigate the uncertainties and challenges we face. It doesn't provide us with neat answers or a formulaic approach, but, crucially, awakens us to the areas where God is at work in us and in the world. It helps us take part in the restoration story, the 'shalom' he is bringing to all things (more on this in chapter 2).

Observation 2

The parable shows the primacy of love. The teacher effectively asks Jesus to sum up everything in Scripture about how to live a good life. The answer Jesus endorses, through Scripture and story, is 'love'. Love God, and love your neighbour as much as yourself.

We know that 'love' is an overused word in our culture – we can love pizza and sunshine, love pets and family members, 'love what you've done with the place' – but stick with us as we unpack what Jesus is getting at here. He's talking about self-sacrificial service, honouring others and wanting their best, even when it's difficult. He's talking about seeing people, all people, as image-bearers of the living God, and treating them accordingly (you may have heard this concept referred to as 'imago Dei'). He's talking about a practical and emotional commitment to the worship of God and the welfare of those around us.

We must learn to love God and love people (including ourselves) first, over everything else. There's a link here to another famous Bible passage about love. In 1 Corinthians 13, Paul writes:

If I have a faith that can move mountains, but do not have love, I am nothing. If I give all I possess to the poor and give over my body to hardship that I may boast, but do not have love, I gain nothing. Love is patient, love is kind . . .[5]

Talk about a challenge! *We could give all we have to the poor, but without love it would mean nothing?* This is so challenging! It can be so easy to look past people in the busyness of the everyday and in trying to get through our to-do lists.

Here lies the key point: activism – all of it, all our action and justice-seeking and striving and serving – has to come from love. For activists, it is more important to learn to love than to set up an amazing project or launch a wildly successful campaign. We *must* keep returning to this idea.

If we can learn to love, then it will ensure we are able to make the right choices when challenges arise, just as we see in the character of the Good Samaritan. He was moved with compassion (the literal translation is 'he was moved in his inward parts'; in everyday English we would say, as *The Message* renders it above, 'his heart went out' to the man), and as a result he took a great personal risk for the benefit of the injured person. In stopping to help instead of hurrying on to safety, he chose to make himself vulnerable to assault by the same robbers who had attacked the Jewish man – and this before he had taken valuable linen, oil and wine from his own stores to dress the victim's wounds, and then paid a large amount of money to ensure he was cared for. He saw the Jewish man's humanity: he loved, and gave of himself accordingly.

A more recent example of a person whose character was shaped by love is Corrie Ten Boom, the watchmaker, writer, and member of the Dutch resistance during the Nazi occupation of the Netherlands. Until the age of 47, she had lived a completely unremarkable life as the world would define it. She lived quietly, worked in her father's clock business and served her local community. By the time the Second World War broke out, she had cultivated such a depth of character that she was able to put herself at great personal risk to help people she had never met before, just like the Good Samaritan. She didn't set out to change the world, but what she did in order to save the lives of her Jewish neighbours was incredible. In her autobiography *The Hiding Place*, published after the war, she shared the wisdom that her father had given her before it: 'Love is the strongest force in the world.'[6] In quietness and ordinariness, she had grown such a profound sense of love for God and others that when the opportunity came to take action, it made all the difference.

How does this happen? How do we 'learn to love'? We put this question to Krish Kandiah, the founder of an adoption and fostering charity, author of *Home for Good*,[7] and adoptive and foster parent to many children. He gave us this analogy:

> Most people, as soon as they find out they're expecting a child, read everything they can. It can be very overwhelming and leave you thinking, 'Oh my goodness, I'm way out of my depth!' Then your child arrives and you feel less prepared than ever. Now you're thinking 'Help! How am I going to do this?!' But there's nothing like the practice of just doing it and learning on the job. It's the commitment to the person, the power of proximity, that forces you to learn. And to continue to learn. I've been a parent for twenty-four years – to over thirty-four children – and I'm still learning.

It's a bit ironic for the first chapter of a book to mention how we need to learn by doing rather than by reading! But it's our hope that these next few chapters will serve as a manual and a handbook as you do just that, rather like the tattered parenting books that I (Rich) still reach for as I work out how to parent my two boys.

Together with the *Hopeful Activists* podcast producer Abi, we've spent the last few years asking activists and theologians questions just like 'How do we learn to love?', and we contacted some of them to get their wisdom in response to this question.

Shane Claiborne, veteran activist, author and new monastic:

> I chose to live in this neighbourhood in Philadelphia where I've been for the last twenty-five years, and it makes a world of difference. The social justice issues become less of a pontificated-upon, calculated thing, and more of a loving response to injustice that is everywhere in our proximity. With so many of these things, until injustice becomes personal or proximate, it's hard to have that fire in your bones. So many of these passions of mine have come out of aspiring to love my neighbour.

Athena Stevens, writer, performer, director, campaigner and social activist:

> I think, for me, I learned to love when I figured out that taking action, rather than remaining complicit in the injustices of the world, was first and foremost an act of love. Every time I describe what is wrong or try to talk to a person and examine their behaviour, it has to be an opportunity to underpin the belief that this individual has dignity and can do better. It's not an opportunity to tear that person down, or to shame or paralyse the individual so that they never do anything productive again. To realise that I am just as f***ed

up as the person or system that I am confronting is to understand that my own humility is a gift given to me by God's grace. And if everything is given by grace, I am able to give love freely, even when it makes me uncomfortable, or my hopes aren't met in this person understanding the harm they are doing.

Chris Lane, church planter in Salford:

Working in the inner city over two decades is a massive honour, but it can be draining at times. Often my friends can have huge ups and downs in their lives, and after making real progress, suddenly everything can fall apart. Walking alongside people can be really hard, sometimes spending many hours over months and years and seeing them find some freedom and healing, only to be cut off without warning. But I am doing this because of love. I experienced the love of Jesus thirty-five years ago, and that love has sustained me through many different challenges in my life since. I have learned to love by experiencing the love of Jesus, not in a one-off experience, but in a daily walk of faith and trust. It is this love that helps me to make sense of the difficult times, this love that gets me out of bed in the morning, this love that softens my heart again and again when I would rather cut myself off in an act of self-protection.

You may want to spend some time yourself, now, reflecting on how God might have been teaching you to 'learn to love' over recent months and years. Where has he been at work?

***

God has unique things for each of us to do. He's already at work, and we have the choice to join in with him. Discerning what these things are – and working out how to take the next steps towards them – is probably why you're reading this book! Over all of these good things he has planned for us, though, love is paramount. After all, as Paul writes in 1 Corinthians, 'these three remain: faith, hope and love. But the greatest of these is love.'[8] Things done in faith, hope and love have the power to last.

What did you write as your response to the reflection question at the start of the chapter? That question – what can I do today that will last into eternity? – is one to which you can keep coming back each day. There are many good things that we can do now, this day, that will have eternal benefit. Foundational in every activity, though, is to learn to love.

Questions for reflection

- When have you experienced the kindness of a stranger? Or when have you observed something similar to this? How did it feel to be shown (or to observe) kindness in this way?
- What reflections did you have on the parable? What questions did it stir up for you? What resonates with you?
- Can you think of people who love well? Does this idea of the primacy of love alter how you view what they do, or how you view any of your own projects or actions?

- How would you explain the concepts of this chapter to someone who hasn't read the book?
- This week, why not try the day-by-day practice of asking Jesus, 'Who should I prioritise today?' Give time for him to drop people or actions into your mind each day and see where he leads.

Recommended resources

- Joyce Huggett, *Hearing Jesus* (Westbury: Eagle, 1999) – out of print but available second-hand
- Corrie Ten Boom, with John and Elizabeth Sherrill, *The Hiding Place* (London: Hodder & Stoughton, 2004)
- Kenneth Bailey, *Jesus through Middle-Eastern Eyes: Cultural studies in the Gospels* (Downers Grove, IL: InterVarsity Press, 2008)
- Shane Claiborne's interview 'Joy vs Injustice: Wisdom for the road', *Hopeful Activists* podcast, 30 August 2019
- Athena Stevens's interview 'Writing the Future: Storytelling, equality and the art of grace', *Hopeful Activists* podcast, 7 June 2019
- Chris Lane's interview 'Miracles, Eating Together and Creating Community', *Hopeful Activists* podcast, 2 July 2021

2

God's grand story

In our Praxis Labs course, we start the session on God's 'grand story' by interviewing an actor. Why would we start a theology discussion by interviewing an actor? Surely a theologian, or at least some form of Christian worker, would be more appropriate?

In order for an actor to perform their role in a play effectively, they need to know both about their character and about the world that he or she lives in. What are the rules of this world? The world of Shakespeare's *Macbeth* is very different from that of Austen's *Pride and Prejudice*, which is entirely different again from George Lucas's *Star Wars* films.

The same is true for us. In order for us to play our role effectively, we likewise need to understand our character – who we are, the unique passions and values God has given us – and the wider story within which we are caught up. Chapter 3 will look at how we can understand more about the unique character God has given each of us, but in this chapter we'll examine the bigger picture.

'In the beginning God created the heavens and the earth'[1] – the beginning to the most-read book in history and, in Christian understanding, the start of *the* story. And, a thousand or so pages later, '"There will be no more death" or mourning or crying or pain . . . I am making everything new!'[2] The end of the story: God renews all things in his great act of re-creation and restoration.

The Bible starts with God's act of loving, good creation. It finishes with healing and renewal. In between, we find ourselves in a world characterised partly by beauty, joy and goodness, and partly by death, sorrow and evil.

The story that is written throughout Scripture is on a grand scale, tracing the creation of the stars to God's restoration of all things at the end of time – and yet there are moments of astounding intimacy. We see God meeting the creation he has made: God speaking to Adam and Eve in the garden; God meeting Elijah in a gentle whisper; God even born into this world. The most mind-blowing example of this loving intimacy between God and people is Jesus: Immanuel, 'God with us'.[3]

In this chapter we're going to dig deeper into God's grand story, exploring its six 'acts' and where we find ourselves in the narrative arc. Before we do, though, take a moment to reflect on the following question: **What do you think was God's original purpose for creation?**

***

One of the key themes we see throughout the Bible is 'shalom', a Hebrew word which is often translated into English as 'peace'. But shalom means more than that. In Scripture, it suggests completeness or wholeness: a set of circumstances where all the complex bits of relationships or situations fall into place. It's a beautiful concept, and one that we don't have an equivalent for in English.

'Shalom' is also used as a verb: to bring shalom is to make something complete, or to restore it.[4] As Krish Kandiah said when we interviewed him, shalom is about everything being rightly related: shalom exists when relationships between God, humans (both our relationships with one another and with ourselves) and the rest of creation function as God intends. Theologian and activist Lisa Sharon Harper (more from her below) has written a whole book exploring what this would look like for relations between nations, between people of different ethnicities, for struggling families, for our relationship with creation, and so on. When we understand that this is what 'peace' means in Scripture, passages such as Isaiah 9 come into sharper focus as they describe Jesus as 'the prince of shalom', whose reign will bring 'shalom without end'.[5]

We're going to use shalom as our lens as we think about the six acts of God's story.

***

The story starts, as we've mentioned, with **Act 1: creation**.[6] The Spirit of God hovers over the waters and breathes into life the universe in all its abundance. We see the sun, moon and stars being formed, land and seas separating, vegetation covering the land, living creatures filling the earth, and the creation of human beings in God's own image. In God's words, this world he has made, in all its completeness and fullness, is *tov me'od*. Translated from Hebrew, this means 'very good'.

This two-word Hebrew phrase has a deeper meaning. As Lisa Sharon Harper explains:

The Hebrews who heard that word in the very beginning would have understood that goodness does not exist inside a created thing itself, but exists *between* things. It's about how we treat each other – about the strength of the relationships in creation. So all of those relationships in creation were *tov me'od*. *Tov* meaning 'good', and *me'od* meaning 'very' – but it's not just 'very', it's forcefully good. God's intention for us is to be in forcefully good relationship with all things.

These forcefully, powerfully good relationships are what characterise God's kingdom; they are what make shalom. In the picture we see here, shalom exists perfectly. The relationships between God, humanity and the rest of creation are defined by their 'good'ness, openness and love. Things are complete.[7]

However, we don't find out much more about this, because things quickly change for the worse in **Act 2: the Fall**, as the relationships start to fracture. The snake speaks to Eve, asking, 'Did God *really* say, "You must not eat from any tree in the garden"?'[8] He twists God's words, sowing distrust. Adam and Eve then eat the fruit from the Tree of the Knowledge of Good and Evil. Lisa shared this insight: 'in Western culture . . . to know something is to understand it intellectually. In the Hebrew culture, however, knowledge was experiential.'[9] To know something was to experience it, to have it affect your life. The fruit from the Tree of the Knowledge of Good and Evil plunges its eaters into an experience of both. But the garden of Eden is already good, already perfect. So as Adam and Eve eat the fruit, choosing not to trust God in the process, the awareness and experience of evil crashes into this previously perfect world. As this happens, we see the breaking of shalom: the relationships between God and humanity, between humans, and between humanity and the rest of creation begin to fall apart. Adam and Eve hide from God; Adam blames Eve for eating the fruit; she in turn blames the snake; and their relationship with the earth becomes one of toil and frustration.

Four relationships have been broken (see Fig. 1).[10]

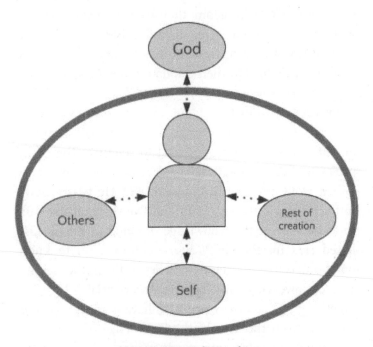

Figure 1 Four relationships

The world is not as it should be, and we each experience the reality of this every day. What can be done?

We proceed to **Act 3: God moving to restore shalom**. We see God getting involved in the world, establishing relationships with people such as Noah and Melchizedek, and forming a specific relationship with Abraham and, later, Israel. One of the key moments in this relationship is the exodus, where we see God hearing the cries of an oppressed people (the Israelites) and responding to the injustice they experience by liberating them – freeing them from the Egyptian Empire.

In the laws God gives the Israelites when they leave Egypt, they are commanded to focus on their relationships with God and with one another. The first four of the Ten Commandments guide their relationship with God: honouring him as their only God, not creating other idols, not misusing his name, keeping the Sabbath holy. The latter six guide their relationships with one another: honouring father and mother, not committing murder, adultery or theft, not lying about neighbours, not coveting things or people that belong to someone else. (We also see here practices that help heal our broken relationship with our sense of self, such as keeping the Sabbath, which literally means 'to rest from work', a practice we sorely need today!) In these commandments, the Israelites are given a pathway towards restored relationships. God also promises them a land[11] where their relationship with the wider creation will be able to be restored. And in the rest of the Pentateuch (Leviticus to Deuteronomy)[12] we see God teaching the people of Israel how to live in the kind of ways that they are meant to live, in order to build shalom.

It's worth noting that the Israelites follow God's commands imperfectly! Throughout the rest of the Old Testament, we see how human beings so often fall short of the way God intends us to live. The Ten Commandments and all the Levitical rules can't change the human heart; something more is needed to restore shalom, to help make the relationships in creation *tov me'od* again. Something more is needed to overcome the death and sorrow that mar this world.

This leads us to **Act 4: Jesus**. In his birth, life, death and resurrection, we see God moving powerfully, sacrificially and lovingly towards his creation. As we mentioned above, Jesus is called Immanuel, meaning 'God with us'; he is the incarnation of the invisible God.[13] Jesus is God knowing what it is like to be human and to be involved in human lives. The Creator chooses to experience his own creation – chooses to have relationship with the human beings he has created, as one of them. In Jesus, we see God's love and restoration in person. He cares about all aspects of the lives of people he meets. He acts in ways that restore people to their families and their homes, through ordinary conversation and through the miraculous. He is the 'prince of shalom'. When we spoke to Sam Wells, vicar of St Martin-in-the-Fields in London, he put it like this:

The Gospels are portraying a purpose of what in Old Testament terms is called shalom – what I might describe as 'being with'. Christ has come to be the embodiment of shalom. Sometimes that involves healings, and sometimes that involves confrontation with authorities.

Throughout his lifetime, Jesus moves to restore relationships between God and humanity, between humans, and between humanity and the rest of the world. He heals people, he provides food and reaches across deep cultural divides, and he challenges those who have benefited from oppressing others. (One of those he challenges, Matthew, goes on to be his disciple. Others, such as the religious leaders, find Jesus' challenge too provocative and plot to kill him.)

It's significant, too, where and when Jesus is born. We spoke to veteran activist, author and new monastic Shane Claiborne about this, and he put it as follows:

What does it mean that at the centre of our faith is a victim of violence, a brown-skinned refugee, born in a manger because there was no room in the inn? Everything about Jesus shows us the solidarity of God with those who are suffering and marginalised, and it's an invitation to lean in – as God has – to the pain and suffering of the world.

This leads us to the crucifixion. We often miss the fact that at first glance, on the afternoon of the first Good Friday, the crucifixion appears to be the triumph of evil over good, death over life. Shane again:

In Jesus, we see this confrontation with principalities and powers but in a way that refused to mirror them, refused to fight on their own terms, and in fact was even offensive and kind of scandalous to his own disciples. They're like, 'No, no, no, kings don't die. Kings kill.' Dying on a cross does not shout out power. But I think that there's something much deeper and more profound that Jesus is doing, which is putting power on display to subvert it with solidarity, with love, with forgiveness, and to show the power of love in contrast to the power of money and hatred and violence.

Sure enough, in his death and resurrection, Jesus completely subverts death and overcomes the powers of evil. It's a victory that has been signposted since the moments just following the Fall, when God spoke to the snake about one of Eve's descendants, and told it:

> he will crush your head,
>   and you will strike his heel.[14]

Jesus overflows with the abundant life of God.[15] Death cannot hold him,[16] and instead, he breaks its power for ever.[17]

In Jesus we see the abundance that is present back in Genesis 1 and 2. Lisa Sharon Harper points out that in our experience 'rivers are made up of small streams that converge. But the four rivers in Eden spring from the garden, then separate and flow outward! This is the essence of abundance: flowing outwards.'[18] Throughout his ministry, we see life flowing out of Jesus. People with leprosy touch him and are healed. A man is set free from demonic possession. A woman who was unable to take part in temple worship because of continual bleeding touches his robe and is restored! In John 4, Jesus says this abundant life is even available to us. Speaking beside a well with a Samaritan woman, who draws some water for him, he says: 'Everyone who drinks this water will be thirsty again, but whoever drinks the water I give them will never thirst. Indeed, the water I give them will become in them a spring of water welling up to eternal life.'[19]

Jesus made it possible for our relationship with God – and everything else – to be fully restored, for shalom to break through, for things to be *tov me'od* again. And the following account in Luke chapter 4 makes it clear that the good news and salvation Jesus brought is for the present as well as the future:

He went to Nazareth, where he had been brought up, and on the Sabbath day he went into the synagogue, as was his custom. He stood up to read, and the scroll of the prophet Isaiah was handed to him. Unrolling it, he found the place where it is written:

'The Spirit of the Lord is on me,
    because he has anointed me
    to proclaim good news to the poor.
He has sent me to proclaim freedom for the
        prisoners
    and recovery of sight for the blind,
to set the oppressed free,
    to proclaim the year of the Lord's favour.'

Then he rolled up the scroll, gave it back to the attendant and sat down. The eyes of everyone in the synagogue were fastened on him. He began by saying to them, 'Today this scripture is fulfilled in your hearing.'[20]

Good news for the poor, freedom for prisoners, recovery of sight for the blind, liberation for oppressed people . . . These are all things we can hope for and see *now*, as well as at the renewal of all things. This is clear from how Jesus lived: Luke 4 goes on to share stories of Jesus casting out demons and healing many people, including the mother-in-law of one of his disciples, Simon. His abundant life – the good news – flows from him and out to many others.

This brings us to **Act 5: where we are now**. Act 5 is a long act. It takes up the whole of the New Testament (apart from bits of Revelation). It's the part of God's story where he is extending shalom to the whole world.

At Pentecost, God's Spirit is poured out on a scared, huddled group of Jesus' followers, and they are transformed. They go and do the things he did: healing ill people, sharing their lives with one another, caring for the poor and the widowed, and challenging the authorities with the truth of Jesus. The apostles take the word of Jesus to the wider world, and the gospel spreads as lives are transformed. Throughout the book of Acts and the letters from Paul, Peter, John, James and others, the members of the early church are called to be witnesses and to make disciples. They are to be transformed, becoming more like Christ. Their relationships with one another, with creation and with God are to change – to become characterised by shalom again.

Our mission and ministry is to be part of that story. It's holistic, all-encompassing, changing every aspect of our lives. We are to seek *tov me'od* relationships with those around us. We are to return to our creation mandate as image-bearers: responsible, accountable for what we do with our lives and how we treat others. It's about working with the Holy Spirit and living out the prayer that Jesus taught us:

Our Father . . .
your kingdom come,
your will be done,
  on earth as it is in heaven.[21]

So where does heaven fit in? Tom Wright, the professor and former Anglican bishop, is fond of saying, 'Heaven is important, but it's not the end of the world!' There's more about this in the book of Revelation, in whose final pages we see **Act 6: shalom being fully restored**. Revelation 21 contains one of my (Rachel's) favourite passages of Scripture:

Then I saw 'a new heaven and a new earth,' for the first heaven and the first earth had passed away, and there was no longer any sea. I saw the Holy City, the new Jerusalem, coming down out of heaven from God, prepared as a bride beautifully dressed for her husband. And I heard a loud voice from the throne saying, 'Look! God's dwelling-place is now among the people, and he will dwell with them. They will be his people, and God himself will be with them and be their God. "He will wipe every tear from their eyes. There will be no more death" or mourning or crying or pain, for the old order of things has passed away.'[22]

Here, the whole of creation is re-created. Everything is renewed, but made even brighter and fuller than before. The Holy City comes down out of heaven from God to populate this new earth, and the promise that we saw in Immanuel, 'God with us', becomes fully real, as God's dwelling-place is 'among the people'. He comforts them, restoring them, ending their grief and pain. The promise of Jesus' resurrection likewise becomes real for God's people, as death is no more. Tom Wright also says: 'Jesus' resurrection is the beginning of God's new project not to snatch people away from earth to heaven but to colonise earth with the life of heaven. That, after all, is what the Lord's Prayer is about.'[23]

The end of the world, then, is not God's people going to heaven to be with him (though this might happen in the meantime), but him (and heaven) coming to earth to be with us. The kingdom of God will be fully present on a renewed earth, and the old order of things – all the corruption, brokenness, death, pain, suffering, waste, bitterness and sin of the world – will go, replaced by true shalom and *tov me'od* relationships. This is the end of the grand story of which we are all a part.

And it's beautiful! This good news – that Jesus is coming back and that he will restore all things – has kept me

(Rachel) going on some dark days. In fact, I suppose that even this 'end' to the story is just the beginning of the rest of the story. As C. S. Lewis put it in *The Last Battle*:

All their life in this world and all their adventures in Narnia had only been the cover and the title page: now at last they were beginning Chapter One of the Great Story which no one on earth has read: which goes on for ever: in which every chapter is better than the one before.[24]

But we're not there yet. Until that time, there will always be brokenness and failure to contend with, that of others and our own. Nevertheless, what we do now resonates into eternity – our efforts can be part of God's restoration project.

The members of the Northumbria Community, mentioned in the previous chapter, are fond of the simple question 'How then shall I live?' In other words, 'In the light of this information, or this understanding of God and the world, how should I live?' It's one small question – with powerfully transformative potential for our relationships with God, the world and people. So, in the light of these six acts, **how then do we live?** You may want to take a moment to reflect on this.

We know we are in Act 5. We know what has gone before – and, crucially, we know the end of the story. But we have to learn how to act, as individuals and in communities. This isn't so much about taking on a character, about striving to be 'the perfect Christian' or adopting 'churchy' social norms; it's more about finding out who we really are, through our relationship with Christ. We are to live as that person – as the people God made us to be. We are to take our places in his story.

We need to experience the wholeness of God in our relationships with one another, with ourselves and with the rest of creation. We need to be filled with the Spirit, following in the footsteps of Jesus. We are called to be a part of bringing shalom – to make the relationships between things *tov me'od* again – and it is a high and beautiful calling.

In the words of Martin Luther King Jr, 'Peace is not merely the absence of tension, but it is the presence of justice.'[25] This is the kind of shalom that characterises God's kingdom: completeness, wholeness, restoration, justice. And this, then, is how we are to live: seeking that shalom in everything we do.

Questions for reflection

- What are your thoughts and feelings about what you've read? Is this the gospel that you've heard preached in your church or elsewhere?
- Was anything totally new or explained in a new way for you? What excited you about it? What challenged you?
- How well rooted in God's story do you think you are? (Is this the story you base your life on?)
- What has helped you to feel rooted, or to see how your life fits with this story? How can you grow deeper roots?

Recommended resources

- Lisa Sharon Harper, *The Very Good Gospel: How everything wrong can be made right* (New York, NY: WaterBrook, 2016)
- N. T. Wright, *Surprised by Hope: Rethinking heaven, the resurrection, and the mission of the Church* (London: SPCK, 2008) and *How God Became King: Getting to the heart of the Gospels* (London; SPCK, 2012)
- Christopher J. H. Wright, *The Mission of God: Unlocking the Bible's grand narrative* (Nottingham: Inter-Varsity Press, 2006)
- René August, *Seeking Peace: Pilgrimage through God's word in God's world with God's people* (Teddington: Tearfund, 2018)
- Scot McKnight, *The Blue Parakeet: Rethinking how you read the Bible* (Grand Rapids, MI: Zondervan, 2008)
- Esau McCaulley, *Reading While Black: African American biblical interpretation as an exercise in hope* (Downers Grove, IL: IVP Academic, 2020)
- Adrian Plass, *Blind Spots in the Bible: Puzzles and paradoxes that we tend to avoid* (Oxford: Bible Reading Fellowship, 2006)
- Jack Wakefield's interview 'Restoration Story: The gardener is back in the garden', *Hopeful Activists* podcast, 17 May 2019

3

What has God put at your core?

In the previous chapter, we stood back to consider the grand sweep of the story that we're all caught up in. Now it's time to zoom in close. In order to get a handle on our – on your – specific role in this story we need to both notice and listen to what God highlights to us, and we each need to understand who he has made us to be as individuals.

This means digging beneath the surface of our circumstances and current opportunities in order to find our true vocation. We asked Shane Claiborne about this, and about the contrasting stories of two tax-collectors we meet in the Gospels: the apostle Matthew and (the famously short) Zacchaeus:

Both of these tax-collectors – their lives are radically changed by Jesus. They're reoriented in how they approach their work, how they approach money. One of them abandons their job, as far as we know. The other stays in his job but turns the system on its head. He becomes a monkey wrench in that system[1] and begins to do exactly the opposite of what it's designed for. He begins to repay people's debt rather than get them entrenched in debt. We don't know how that story ends, but what's important is that they are both seeking this new way of living: a countercultural lifestyle from the world that they were in.

Two tax-collectors; two very different paths after encountering Jesus. Just because our outward circumstances look similar doesn't mean that Jesus calls us to follow him in the same way. Shane pointed us to this verse in Paul's letter to the Romans: 'Do not conform to the pattern of this world, but be transformed by the renewing of your mind.'[2] He reflected:

We see that kind of transformation in the story of these two young disciples. But nonconformity to the world doesn't mean uniformity. It doesn't mean that we're all going to live the same kind of countercultural narrative or make the same decisions. We have this imagination that we're invited into. There are some consistencies – for example, we're to be near to the poor, we are to hold our possessions differently, we're to be non-violent people; but while those values are radically countercultural, they're not a uniform antidote for how every person has to live their life. Not everyone's going to volunteer in a soup kitchen. Not everyone's going to build a house with Habitat for Humanity or ring the bell of the Salvation Army. We're all going to find our way a little differently. But at the centre of that is this radical call of Jesus and the urgent struggle of our neighbours.

So how do we find our role? You may have heard it said that the key to it is identifying where 'what we're good at' overlaps with 'what the world needs'.[3] There's some truth in this, and we'll return to thinking about our gifts and skills at the end of this chapter, but as you can see from what Shane has said above, finding our role is clearly a much deeper process than that. (And in any case, the area of overlap isn't that narrow: there's a lot of brokenness in the world, and we can use our skills to bring restoration in lots of different ways.)

Instead, we think understanding our role goes hand in hand with God restoring our connection to ourselves (one of the broken relationships we talked about in chapter 2). It's a process of self-discovery: uncovering the unique reflection of the image of God that he has placed in you. The first step often lies in uncovering the values God has placed at your core.

Let us explain. If we dig under the surface of our daily activities, conversations and relationships, we find that each of us is leading our life according to a set of core values (or principles) that influence how we make the biggest decisions in life. Often, we're not even consciously aware of them. Looking back on my teens and early twenties, I (Rich) can see now that many of my decisions were influenced by an underlying value around status, around looking good. I would never have said that **status** was a core value that I held, but I wanted to go to a prestigious university, and then I took a job in the civil service that sounded cool (even if it was about working for the greater good). I don't think I was conscious of it at the time, but status was a value that I had inherited from the world or from people close to me, and it was unwittingly influencing some very big decisions.

A similarly common value in our society is **security** (the desire to have things neatly arranged to guarantee our well-being into the future). I know a few people whose parents really advocated for this value in their career and life choices, and although this wasn't my experience, it was probably in the background to some extent, gently imbibed from my culture without my realising it.

Status and security are not core values for the person God has made me to be, and I distinctly remember the moment when I was able to call them out as such. My wife Sophie and I were living in London, and on a visit to Brockwell Park Lido I scrawled a poem on the back of a paper napkin, unpicking the values I saw being lived out all around me. Part of it reads:

High wages, secure
final salary pensions, houses
Security. Prestige.
What on earth are we living for?
Not this.
You've cracked this glass.
It's wafer thin
And I can see what's beneath.

When we live out of line with our true, core values it creates a sense of disconnect, of discomfort or even agitation.

Around the same time, Sophie and I were spending quite a lot of time 'passion mapping': taking big sheets of paper and individually writing down all the things that made us feel alive, that we felt passionate about and drawn to, and then trying to group them into themes. For a while, we had these huge sheets of paper hung up on the wall in our flat so we could add to them easily! Three core values emerged from this process for me: **adventure**, **helping people find freedom**, and **beauty**. Underpinning these three was a strong core value around the presence of God.

Adventure is pretty close to being the opposite of security, and freedom doesn't sit well with status either (which often requires you to play by the rules). So my true core values were in firm opposition to those that I had unwittingly imbibed.

Exercise 1. If discerning core values is a new concept for you, you may already be buzzing with questions about what those values might be in your case. You may also be feeling uneasy about the suggestion that you could be living in a way that doesn't line up with your true values (I mean, who would live according to a value such as 'status', right? Ha!). So, to help you ground this idea of values in your own life, we've worked with two life coaches – Anna Boocock of Connect2Coaching and Nick Smith of Square Pegs Coaching – to shape some reflection questions about it, which are scattered throughout this chapter.[4] Here are the first two:

- **What were your main caregivers' values around what 'a life well lived' looks like?**

- **What did the culture you grew up in tell you about what 'a life well lived' looks like?**

***

Our values sit at a level deeper than specific causes or issues, even though they may be connected to them. They help to shape what makes us feel alive, what inspires us and what makes us angry.

For me, they explained why, after a few years, I was getting restless in my civil service job! I had learned a lot, but working in a big bureaucracy isn't exactly the epitome of adventure. Or take beauty, another of my core values. As I'm writing this chapter, the sun is setting outside the window. I've just stopped for a few moments to take it in, open the window, and simply look and be restored. Beauty inspires me. By contrast, the marring of beauty, the marring of the image of God in other human beings, makes me incredibly angry. This connects to the value I hold around freedom, and helping others to find it. Whatever I do, it *has* to be connected to this; indeed, this value has influenced pretty much every job, voluntary role or piece of activism I've ever pursued.

In Scripture, we sometimes see a person's core value being named – literally – through the giving of a new name. Jesus gives the apostle Simon the name Peter, which means 'rock', calling out the strength that is perhaps the true, redeemed nature of Peter's confidence and impetuousness. And in Acts 4 a man from Cyprus is renamed Barnabas by the apostles, meaning 'son of encouragement', perhaps reflecting part of his true nature and describing how he often behaved.

Wherever we find ourselves, our values shape how we act. Jan de Villiers is the founder of youth charity e:merge and the social enterprise Futurekraft, which has helped incubate and develop more than 150 justice projects, particularly around Bradford.[5] He describes three of his core values as 'fatherhood, authenticity and freedom'. Whatever he's working on, these values drive his approach:

> In my desire to do stuff and change the world it's not so much about the projects I tackle; it's about these core values. Whatever the project, they will drive my approach. So for example, fatherhood for me is about enabling others. Supporting people, helping others to do their thing, is what drives me.

Wherever he finds himself, supporting and releasing others tends to become a major focus of his time.

I (Rich) had the pleasure of working with Jan when I lived in Bradford, and this value really comes across in how he lives and works. It clearly goes to his core and is something he's tapped into, revealing the unique reflection of the image of God in him. You may also have met people who have this same sense to them – that they are really living in line with the person God made them to be. I remember another time, at a small gig performed by the musician Rob Halligan, when I felt, 'Wow, this guy is absolutely doing what he was made to do.' There was a sense of pure shalom about it that you could feel in the room.

In my case, I've realised that in a 'work' context, my value of adventure sits pretty close to pioneering, and that's why I inevitably find myself starting new projects (perhaps occasionally to the exasperation of my colleagues!). In my role in the Global Advocacy Team at Tearfund I have the freedom and opportunity to do this, but it's not compulsory – not everyone in my role is always starting new projects (thank goodness). But that's what I find myself doing, because that's a reflection of who I am. As I remarked to a colleague a couple of years ago, 'Without adventure, I don't feel alive.'[6] Indeed, Anna (one of our life coaches) likes to challenge people with a quote commonly attributed to the pastor and civil rights activist Howard Thurman, an advisor to Martin Luther King: 'Don't ask what the world needs. Ask what makes you come alive, and go do it because what the world needs is people who have come alive.' Living in line with our core values – operating out of our deepest self – is part of experiencing life in all its fullness.

Exercise 2. Here's another exercise that we were introduced to by Anna and Nick, with the purpose of helping you to discover your values. Your values have always been with you; they show up in the films you love, the people you admire, your strong emotions such as anger and joy, the music you listen to, the books you read, the art you enjoy. Often our best moments come when our values are honoured either by ourselves or by others. Our worst moments come when our values are trampled on or ignored. Consider these questions:

- **Who inspires you? What is it about them that you are drawn to?**

- **What most excites you in life? In your work or volunteering? At home? In your leisure time?**
- **What is your favourite film / book / quote / song lyric? What draws you to it? What resonates with you?**
- **What makes you angry? What are your 'soapbox' issues? What are you prepared to suffer or make sacrifices for?**

Identifying our values is a lifelong process, and it's certainly going to take you longer than five minutes and a few scribbled notes in the margin of this page. But hopefully these questions will help start a process of self-discovery for you (or remind you to revisit this area if it's something you've worked on in the past). You might even consider spending some time with a trusted friend or a life coach, such as Anna and Nick, talking through these questions.

***

Let's briefly return now to thinking about our skills and talents, which are also part of finding our role.

If we were asked what we were good at when we left school, we'd probably say something like 'good at maths, bad at writing essays' or 'good at sports, bad at geography'. These are valid answers, but the lessons we were taught in school don't necessarily equip us with skills such as listening well, helping others solve problems, running a project, negotiating a compromise or being able to manage a budget.

Earlier today, I (Rich) asked Aidan and Nathaniel about this book and what they thought it meant to be a 'real super-goodie' (that's how I described the book for a 7-year-old and a 4-year-old – 'It's all about how to be a real super-goodie' – because obviously that's what a hopeful activist is!). Their answers revolved around love and kindness. At its most foundational, the skills we all need to learn are kindness and love. (This reminds me of the bit in the book *The Boy, the Mole, the Fox and the Horse* when the mole asks the boy, 'What do you want to be when you grow up?' The boy's answer? 'Kind.')[7] However, there are a host of other skills that we might have: drawing, negotiating, persuasive writing, organising, managing a project, listening, dancing, knowing your way around a spreadsheet, cooking, speaking a different language or working cross-culturally, to name just a few. All of these can be put to work in the service of love and kindness.

How do we truly work out where our strengths lie? This has a lot in common with how we started working out our core values earlier on in the chapter. We need to take time to notice and observe ourselves. What did you spend lots of time doing as a child? What are you most keen to learn now? What do you notice you pick up quickly? What are the things that others notice about you and speak highly of? The researcher and author Marcus Buckingham describes a strength as something that 'draws you in, makes time fly by . . . and makes you feel strong'.[8]

These things may in fact be connected. In my case (Rachel), I spent a lot of time when I was younger with my nose buried in a book. (I particularly loved fantasy books and was quite proud of the fact that I finished the last Harry Potter book just after 4 a.m. on the night it came out!) I love to find myself fully absorbed in another world, or another place or time. I went on to study literature at university and learned a lot about writing in the process, and now my work is wrapped up in the written word, both writing things myself and copy-editing others' work.

Reading so many different stories also exposed me to lots of different perspectives on the world. Studies have suggested that reading fiction makes people more empathetic,[9] and I've certainly noticed that I have a habit of picking up on what others are feeling (sometimes that's a really helpful thing; other times, not so much!). I'm told by friends and family that I'm a good listener too, which was definitely developed through training at my former job, but it also draws on some of that empathy I picked up when I was younger.

Our skills and talents can grow and change; they are far less 'permanent' than our core values, though there certainly will be links.

Exercise 3. Take time now to look over the following questions, and jot down your answers.

- What did you spend lots of time doing as a child?
- What are you most keen to learn now? What do you notice you pick up quickly?
- What are the things that others notice about you and speak highly of?
- Where could you use these things in God's grand story?

***

When we cover values in our Praxis Labs course, sometimes we're challenged by participants who feel that this focus on values is self-indulgent. With so many people in the world struggling even to survive, is it right to spend this amount of time thinking about 'self-actualisation' when we could just get out there and get on with it?

There are definitely times when we just need to get off our bums and do something. But time spent looking inwards with God is not a waste. In fact, we would argue it's an essential discipline for activists, and is about taking seriously the instruction in the book of Romans that Shane mentioned at the start of this chapter: 'Do not conform to the pattern of this world, but be transformed by the renewing of your mind.'[10] Time spent discovering the deepest reaches of the person God has made us to be – and resisting becoming the person the world pressures us to be – actually allows us to better work with him in his mission in the world, and to play our role in his grand story.

Working for transformation is hard, so if you want to be effective and stay the course, it will really help if your activism aligns with your core values, with the things that give you life. (More on this when we discuss burnout in chapter 9.) More fundamentally, what God wants for everyone is for them to uncover and embrace the fullness of the human being he has made them to be. This is ultimately the shalom that we are working for – for everyone to find those restored relationships with God, themselves, those around them and creation. If this is truly what we want, then we have to be able to model it in our own lives. The more we are able to live in line with our core values, the more we are likely to be able to help others to do the same.

There are lots of ways of taking this idea even deeper. Over the last few years, I (Rich) have really appreciated the Enneagram framework as a way of exploring more about who I am with God and how to be most fully my 'true self' (more resources on this are signposted below). We also know a lot of activists (including ourselves) who have really benefited from counselling; in fact, 'Get counselling' is a piece of advice that we've heard several times from people we've interviewed on the *Hopeful Activists* podcast! Going on retreat is another practice that we hold in very high regard.

The older we get, the more we realise that the 'renewing of our minds' mentioned in Romans is a lifelong process of transformation. The late author Ruth Bell Graham, who is best known as the wife of the evangelist Billy Graham, knew that her life was one long journey of becoming the person she was meant to be in Jesus. The inscription on her tombstone reads: 'End of Construction – thank you for your patience'. What a beautiful way of expressing the growth and change that happens in us over a lifetime!

Questions for reflection

- Having named some of the values from your upbringing, how well do they sit with you now? Which do you want to hold on to, or let go of?
- Having started to explore the things that inspire you, excite you and make you angry, do you have any thoughts about what your core values might be?

Recommended resources

- Karen Walrond, *The Lightmaker's Manifesto: How to work for change without losing your joy* (Minneapolis, MN: Broadleaf Books, 2021)
- Anna Boocock's life-coaching resources: connect2coaching.org
- Nick Smith's life-coaching resources: SquarePegsCoaching.com
- Ian Morgan Cron and Suzanne Stabile, *The Road Back to You: An Enneagram journey to self-discovery* (Downers Grove, IL: InterVarsity Press, 2016)
- The Enneagram Institute: www.enneagraminstitute.com
- Skye Jethani, *With: Reimagining the way you relate to God* (Nashville, TN: Thomas Nelson)

4

What is God giving you hope for?

Having looked at the overarching plan of God's grand story in chapter 2 and started thinking through our core values in chapter 3, we're now going to look at another way to identify the areas where God is calling us to devote our time, effort and energy. We'll be exploring the nature of hope with activist and development practitioner Thobekile Ncube and human rights and gender equality campaigner Naureen Akhtar. We will think through the question of where God might be prompting you to get involved in the issues around you, and we're also going to touch a little on how to keep hoping when it's hard – though we'll dig into that more in chapter 9.

'Hope' is an odd word in the English language. When we use it in sentences such as 'I hope it'll be sunny tomorrow', or 'I hope that the exam goes well for you', or 'I hope the train won't be delayed', there's always an element of uncertainty. We don't know whether the weather will do what we want it to do, whether the exam will have the questions we want or whether the trains will run on time.

When we read of hope in the Bible, though, it's quite different. Hope is tied to God's promises and his character. In the Old Testament, the Israelites in Egypt hoped to see the promised land; in the letters of the early church in the New Testament, Christians hoped for the new creation to come. The letter to the Hebrews says, 'We have this hope as an anchor for the soul, firm and secure.'[1] The writer is referring to the promises that we explored in chapter 2: the restoration of the relationships between God, humanity and creation. Hope like this – dependent on God, on his character and on the promises he has made – is of a very different kind from the hope we usually talk about.

This leads us on to our reflection question for this chapter. In Hebrews 11, the writer says that 'faith is the substance of things hoped for'.[2] In other words, faith is visible. It's the activity that reflects the promises of God that haven't yet been fulfilled. Our activity will spring from the hope that we have. Or, to paraphrase Rubem Alves, the Brazilian theologian: 'Hope is hearing the melody of the future. Faith is having the courage to dance to it now.'[3] So . . . **what does God's future sound like to you?**

***

Now, there are many good answers to the above question! You may have thought of something further off (such as the restoration of all creation), something that feels like a mountain to climb (such as seeing change in unjust political systems) or something closer to home (such as being able to plant and grow a community garden). Keep hold of those thoughts, as we are going to explore them in a minute.

First, though, let's go back 2,500 years, to a valley full of human bones, and a man wandering around amid them.

It's described in Ezekiel 37, and it's a place from which I (Rich) have learned a lot about hope:

> The hand of the LORD was on me, and he brought me out by the Spirit of the LORD and set me in the middle of a valley; it was full of bones. He led me to and fro among them, and I saw a great many bones on the floor of the valley, bones that were very dry. He asked me, 'Son of man, can these bones live?'
>
> I said, 'Sovereign LORD, you alone know.'
>
> Then he said to me, 'Prophesy to these bones and say to them, "Dry bones, hear the word of the LORD! This is what the Sovereign LORD says to these bones: I will make breath enter you, and you will come to life. I will attach tendons to you and make flesh come upon you and cover you with skin; I will put breath in you, and you will come to life. Then you will know that I am the LORD."'
>
> So I prophesied as I was commanded. And as I was prophesying, there was a noise, a rattling sound, and the bones came together, bone to bone. I looked, and tendons and flesh appeared on them and skin covered them, but there was no breath in them.
>
> Then he said to me, 'Prophesy to the breath; prophesy, son of man, and say to it, "This is what the Sovereign LORD says: come, breath, from the four winds and breathe into these slain, that they may live."' So I prophesied as he commanded me, and breath entered them; they came to life and stood up on their feet – a vast army.

> Then he said to me: 'Son of man, these bones are
> the people of Israel. They say, "Our bones are dried up
> and our hope is gone; we are cut off."'[4]

God leads Ezekiel back and forth in a valley full of bones,
making sure he has a good look at them. Then he asks him,
'Can these bones live?'

Why does God ask this question? I've pondered this for
a long time. It's odd! Bones are the remnants of something
long dead; they embody and symbolise death. Additionally,
God should know the answer to this seemingly impossible
question. He is, after all, God: all-knowing and all-powerful,
the Creator who saw the end from the beginning. Surely he
knows whether it is possible for these bones to live.

God knows the answer, but I think that he cares what
Ezekiel thinks. It matters what Ezekiel thinks about this
issue because God wants to give Ezekiel a role in bringing
restoration and renewal in this place of death. Instead
of being a neutral observer or an interested onlooker,
Ezekiel has the opportunity to be an active participant.
But he's unlikely to participate if he has no hope for these
bones! I think that's why the question matters: hope is a
prerequisite for action. As we wrote earlier, 'Our activity
will spring from the hope that we have.' No hope equals
no action.

So God asks, 'Can these bones live?', and Ezekiel
responds, 'Sovereign LORD, you alone know.' We can read
Ezekiel's answer in two ways: either 'Of course they can, if
you want them to', or 'I really don't know, but you're asking
me, so maybe?' Either way, he has enough hope that when

God seeks to involve him, he is willing to speak life to the bones and be part of God's plan to work the impossible in that place. The bones come together and stand up on their feet, forming a vast army.

This passage speaks to me about the tension at the heart of hope. We have an eternal hope for restoration and renewal, as described in the first section of this chapter. But sometimes God also gives us specific hope for particular instances of renewal in our time. In fact, I think that we often need this. Without it we wouldn't start working on many of the injustices we see today; they just look too big, too intractable (just as I imagine the struggle against apartheid, or for free education, or for women to have the vote, looked decades ago to those who faced those issues). God takes us to a valley of dry bones and gives us hope that something just might be possible there.

Let me introduce Thobekile ('Thobes' for short!) Ncube, a frequent contributor to our Praxis Labs course and one of the most inspiring activists I know. Thobes has spent many years walking alongside marginalised people and activists in southern Africa, sometimes at significant personal risk, and she has accumulated a lot of wisdom in the process.

Thobes pointed out to me that, in this passage, the end result surpasses even what God speaks about at the beginning. At the start, the question is whether the bones can live, not whether they can become a huge army, but that's what we end up with. God does immeasurably more than he indicated might happen or that Ezekiel could have imagined.

I've worked on projects where this has been the case, and I've also worked on projects that haven't turned out as I hoped they would. Navigating this tension between our sure hope that all things will one day be made new, and the hope for specific instances of restoration in the present, is at the heart of what it means to be a hopeful activist.

For now, though, you may want to consider whether God is leading you to a particular valley at the moment. Thobes made another interesting point about this passage: it's clear that 'the hand of the Lord is on Ezekiel'. When we feel that God is at work, we sometimes assume that he's going to take us somewhere amazing, but God shows Ezekiel something that is difficult. He takes him to a hard place: a valley full of dry bones.

Why not take a moment to read the passage through again, and sit with the question: **God, what is the valley of dry bones you are taking me to?**

***

Sometimes we have a clear sense of calling in answer to the above question, but sometimes not. Often it takes time and discernment to figure it out (we talk more about the people you need around you to help with this in chapter 8). We asked Thobes for her advice on discerning God's call:

One of the ways is looking back on your life. Are there things you cannot shut up about, no matter how many times you've been asked to be quiet or told it doesn't matter? Where are the areas that, even from a young age, you cared deeply about? Make a note of those things! If you wanted to do advocacy around climate change, for example, the way you will do it is unique to you. God wants you to bring what he's given you into that field.

Then, think through: what are the things that make me extremely very angry (as we say in Zimbabwe)? What are the things that whenever you look at them, you ask 'Why does this happen?'

Thobes shared a few examples of the things that have sparked anger for her: trees being cut down; children not being allowed to play; governments committing gross human rights violations and then everyone carrying on as though it's normal. 'Think of the things that when you see them in the papers or on the news, you find yourself getting angry. It's an indication that you've got enough energy – because anger is energy – about that issue to push through.'

Of course, anger is not the only type of energy we might feel, as Thobes explains:

It might even be that you're not angry about an issue, but that when you engage with it, your heart is filled with joy. Whether someone is giving you money to do it or not, you would do it. Maybe you talk lots with your family about it, and engaging them in conversation makes you happy. This is an indication that you should go with it! I am convinced that God does not want us to be fuelled by just anger. He doesn't hate it when that happens, but if we engage with the things he's put in our hearts – the aspect of his heart for justice that he has given us – then he knows it's going to fulfil us, as we join our heart with his.

The key thing here is to *notice* what is going on in your life and your heart. Sometimes it's obvious, but other times we need to slow down and take some time out to notice these things. It might be worth taking a day or a few days on retreat, to think and pray over these questions, and then talk them over with a couple of trusted friends.

Let's take some time now, though, to reflect: on the needs, causes and ideas that we are currently involved in; on those that we feel God might be highlighting to us; and on those that excite us. Remember that this is not all about *what* we do. As we discussed in the introduction, *why* and *how* we do things – holding on to the primacy of love – is at least as important.

We're going to do this by using a mind map. Take a large sheet of paper. On one side of the paper write down all the needs, causes and ideas you're involved with at the moment. These could be big or small: being involved in Extinction Rebellion, or meeting your local MP to talk about unfair cuts to Universal Credit. It could be your local parenting group, or even a hobby. You might have lots of things to write, or maybe just one or two. I (Rachel) had a go, and my page looks a little like Figure 2.

Now, on another sheet, write down some of the things that Thobes mentioned: the needs, causes and ideas that make you angry or that give you joy. The things that stir your heart for justice and that you just can't stop talking about!

What is God giving you hope for?

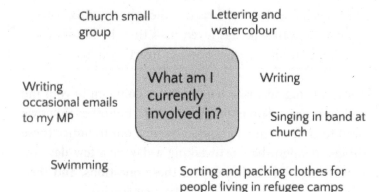

Figure 2 Rachel's mind map, part 1

The things that the Holy Spirit keeps giving you a little nudge about or that you've hoped for for many years. You have permission to write everything down; don't rule anything out at this stage. Mine looks like Figure 3.

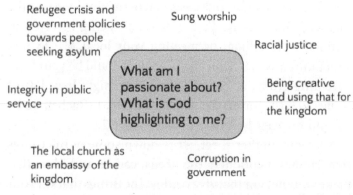

Figure 3 Rachel's mind map, part 2

How well does your current activity match up with what you are passionate about? You may have found that there is a great deal of overlap, which is great! Or you may have found that there is a bit of overlap – that you are doing some things (such as writing to your MP; see my example in Fig. 2) that link to the things you care about (such as government policies towards people seeking asylum – one of my examples in Fig. 3). You may even have found that there is very little overlap.

Having written down the things that have been on your heart for a long time, turn to God and ask him whether there is something in them he would like you to pursue or think more about. Take some time to reflect on the following questions:

- **What are the dreams here?**
- **What are the unresolved questions?**
- **What are the things you want to think and pray more about?**

***

A key question that we often have to answer after an exercise like this is: 'How do I know when I should stop doing something that I'm currently involved in, to make space for something new?' We wish there were a simple formula for answering this question effectively! It's a good question to ask regularly, to ensure that we don't become stuck in a rut, but not so often that we are constantly chopping and changing when things get hard.

These are some of the things that we've found helpful to consider:

- Have you spoken to wise friends and family about your thoughts? What did they say?
- Are there people around you whom you can join in with? Or have people joined in with *you* as you've sought to involve them in what you're doing?
- Have the resources that you need started to come in? (Examples are finances, physical space, technology or other materials.) There may not be lots – maybe it will be something small. Thobes shared: 'I've not seen God start with huge amounts of resources with people, but there will be some. Then it grows as he grows the resources, money, people and material you need.'
- Have you had any 'divine appointments'? Maybe you met someone on a train or at church who happens to have been having similar thoughts recently, or an old friend got in touch out of the blue.

This isn't to say that if the people, resources and divine appointments aren't happening, the thing you're doing isn't what God wants you to do. Think of all the prophets in the Old Testament who had to go it alone. Thobes added:

When you step out, sometimes support might not come. But God will have done other things that make you certain that he wants you to do this. So, you go through a period of isolation: just you, and him, and the dream. Who knows what he's doing? At the time, it doesn't make sense – but I think he's depositing what you need, to then be able to implement what it is you want when the time is right. Sometimes, it might be that you're doing the right thing – it's just not yet time.

So, in those periods of isolation, when things don't go the way we want them to and we're feeling disappointment, how do we hold on to hope?

We spoke to Naureen Akhtar, a human rights activist and gender equality campaigner in Pakistan, shortly after the devastating floods that hit that country in 2022. Millions had been left homeless and without drinking water, and almost 1,700 people died. With these things exacerbating some of the already challenging issues Naureen was working on, we asked her this question. She shared:

I was thinking, 'Why is God allowing this? Why is there injustice?' The question is always there in my mind. I ask God directly, 'Why?' But deep down, there is always a voice that I hear that gives me hope, of God telling us clearly: 'You do your best and I will take care of the rest myself.' He's God! He's the Creator. There is always hope.

Naureen's connection to God – her ability to hear his voice in the midst of crisis, to sense God's reassurance – and her knowledge of his character gives her hope for the future.

Thobes concurred:

The thing about being in it for the long haul . . . It's less about holding on to the promises and more about holding on to the giver of the promise. When I say 'holding on to the giver of the promise', it gives the idea that I'm the one who's holding on to God, but I have found that he's the one who holds on to you. You live in the consciousness of being held by him. So when things hit the fan, and it does not make sense, there's every fact suggesting that God couldn't have promised what he has done . . . you need to be in that space where you are held by him, remembering his character, who he is: he doesn't lie.

Over time, your experience of hopeful activism might shift. That's fine! Over her years working with marginalised communities, hope has evolved for Thobes too:

Initially, before I'd been pushed down a few times by not getting results, hope was having a picture of what we wanted to see and being certain that we would see it – in the next month, in six months' time, or (in the development world) in the three-year cycle of projects. Hope was being sure that the things we would do in year two would lead to the results we wanted to see in year three. When that didn't happen, hope had to shift from things that were dependent on us, from things that you could see and touch, to the promises that God gave about the thing we hoped to see.

This goes back to the tension that we talked about earlier in this chapter: discerning when God is calling us to hold on to hope for a specific instance of restoration now, and when he isn't. (Perhaps he's simply asking us to live in the light of the longer-term promise of restoration.) Here's one example of how this is playing out for me (Rich) right now.

At the time of writing, I'm in the final stages of a project trying to get large companies to do more to respect the human rights of workers at the end of their plastics value chains – the women and men who collect 60% of all the plastic that gets recycled globally but who often receive very low pay and work in dangerous conditions. The team and I have called out these companies in the media, and we've also worked to bring them into touch with the voices and perspectives of the very people who are affected. It's one of the hardest projects I've ever worked on, hugely tiring and draining, and it's almost collapsed many times. Humanly speaking, you could compare it to a house of cards which could fall apart at any moment, even as we seek to place the last two cards on the top.

But when I talk to God about it, I sense that these bones can live. Sometimes, I'm completely confident that he will bring it to completion; at other times, I waver. But I sense that he's at work, and I can't deny that we've seen God pull the project through crisis after crisis, sometimes pretty miraculously. Without the hope that he will do so again, I would have thrown in the towel many times. [And, indeed, a few months after I wrote this, the project *did* come to fruition with the launch of the Fair

Circularity Initiative (faircircularity.org) by four of the world's largest companies, convened by my employer, Tearfund.]

Naureen also shared with us how looking back and reflecting on the change that has happened in the past can be helpful when facing challenges in the present. Reflecting on her work for women's rights in Pakistan, she spoke inspiringly:

We have seen change. I remember when I was a child, thirty years ago, the situation was different. I remember many women activists and community workers, including my mother and my few aunties, who really worked in this country to achieve what we are enjoying today. In the 1990s, women were not allowed to move without covering their head. The women in this country had a long struggle, and the fruit of their struggle is what we are now enjoying. We have freedom to move, freedom to work, freedom to choose what we want to do. We have freedom even to have a dialogue with men, sitting at the table with them. I strongly hope that women of my age will take on what they have started, so that the young girls and many others who are still to be born will have a just, full, vibrant and healthy society where all will be equal. This is what I dream. And this is what gives me hope.

So, 'What is God giving you hope for?' Thobes had one more bit of brilliant wisdom to share:

Hope has become, for me, being absolutely certain that – in regard to the thing I'm passionate about, that I'm burning for, that keeps me up at night – God is more interested in it than I will ever be.

If we go back to Ezekiel 37, I think we can see this – I can feel God's excitement growing as the restoration takes place. When he initially tells Ezekiel to speak to the bones, he says: 'Prophesy to these bones and say to them . . .' Then a few verses later, as the renewal is under way, it's 'Prophesy to the breath; prophesy, son of man, and say to it . . .' When I hear that voice in my mind I can feel the extra energy the second time round! The command is repeated: 'Prophesy, prophesy, son of man!'

In regard to the things I'm passionate about, my heart burns because he causes it to burn; because he is more interested in it, it will come to pass. So hope has become about desiring the changes we want to see, but also being at peace with it not happening while I am alive. I may not be able to see any indication that this is about to happen. In fact, it might look like it's going the other way. But I'm going to hold on. I'm going to trust that it will happen, because he said so. I am not greater than God, so I cannot care for an issue more than he does.

Questions for reflection

- What does God's future sound like to you?
- Ask God: 'What is the valley of dry bones you are taking me to?'
- What are your dreams?

- What are your unresolved questions?
- Are there any things you need to think and pray about more?

You may find it helpful to reflect on the following questions, and then read chapter 9, 'Love and (how to avoid) burnout'.

- Have you been disappointed in the past? How have you handled it?
- How can you rely on God in the midst of disappointment and challenge?

Recommended resources

- Shane Claiborne, *The Irresistible Revolution: Living as an ordinary radical* (Grand Rapids, MI: Zondervan, 2016)
- Lynda Sterling's interview 'Look Again Artist: Fridges have feelings', *Hopeful Activists* podcast, 5 July 2019
- Naureen Akhtar's interview 'Human Rights in Pakistan', *Hopeful Activists* podcast, 12 March 2021

5

Handling power

Over the past few chapters, we've talked a fair bit about our attitudes towards ourselves and towards God. In this chapter we're going to explore a bit more of what we touched on in the introduction: the primacy of love, and what it looks like, in our interactions with others.

I'm guessing that part of what got you thinking about activism in the first place was a concern for others. But have you ever thought through how to turn that concern into healthy action – action that has love for others at its heart?

We heard from Thobes Ncube in the previous chapter. Having spent years working with marginalised communities, she has more experience than most in walking with vulnerable people:

> A lot of the time, things have happened in people's lives that mean they have lost their voice, or can't use it any more. I want people to find the freedom to be fully who God called them to be; to fully function in the things that are in their heart.

Finding the freedom to be fully who God called them to be . . . Isn't that an awesome picture? This is the journey that all of us are on – finding our true, God-given identity and our true vocation (as we discussed in chapter 3).

In this chapter, we're going to hear a bit more from Thobes, and we're also going to chat to Sam Wells, the author, theologian, and vicar of St Martin-in-the-Fields near Trafalgar Square in London. He has spent a lot of time reflecting on different ways of acting and being around those we see as vulnerable through his ministry with those who are homeless (a big focus for St Martin-in-the-Fields). We first spoke to him for an episode of the *Hopeful Activists* podcast back in 2019. He shared with us his framework for our activity (see Table 1).

Table 1 Examples of ways of acting and being around those who are homeless

Working for	*Being for*
For example: Setting up an organisation to help people who are homeless – maybe running a soup kitchen or giving donations of clothes	For example: Writing blogs online highlighting how people experiencing homelessness are treated in the UK, tweeting at MPs/companies/councils to ask for change
Working with	*Being with*
For example: Pulling together a group of interested parties (those who are homeless, local business leaders, local councillors, volunteer groups, churches, mosques, etc.), to discuss together what can be done to address the issue	For example: Sitting down with someone experiencing homelessness and having a cup of tea – maybe discussing the Premier League or whether we need a new prime minister!

The four approaches laid out in the table have different strengths and weaknesses (and our activism doesn't always fall neatly into one of these boxes). 'Working for' might be an effective way of getting stuff done, but there's something that doesn't quite sit right about this if our aim is truly for everyone to find the freedom to be fully the person God calls them to be. Operating in this way might mean not even speaking to someone experiencing homelessness before acting! In one of the examples given (setting up a soup kitchen), the person running the soup kitchen has all the decision-making capacity: what flavour soup is served; whether there are bits of extra food provided; what time and how often the kitchen runs. A person experiencing homelessness has limited or no choice in what is provided for them – they might not like the soup provided, or the kitchen could run at an inconvenient time. As Sam shared, 'A person "working for" has created a structure where all the assets are on their side of the relationship, and all the deficits are on the other person's side.'

In contrast, 'working with' acknowledges that someone experiencing homelessness is part of a network of relationships that need to be restored, that they have a voice and that they should have influence over things that affect their lives. Any action to address the issue may be slower to get going (needing, as it does, to take into account more voices and different perspectives), but it is action that seeks to give equal dignity – equal assets – to all those involved. In the example we've used, 'working with' would mean ensuring that people experiencing homelessness were part of the decision-making team running the soup kitchen. They would be involved in deciding what is offered, providing the food and other amenities, and – in fact – deciding whether a soup kitchen is what is actually required at all!

'Being for' combines the problems of 'for' with the difficulties of 'being' (more on that below). You don't necessarily have to speak to someone experiencing homelessness to be 'for' them. Raising awareness of an issue using online platforms is sometimes helpful. But if it is not backed up with action, then online words, tweets, posts and videos can be empty; they're effectively asking others to take necessary action instead.

'Being with' is different again. Sam reflected:

Activists often find 'being with' very challenging, because they like to use their skills, and they like to be busy. They tend to describe 'being with' as being too passive. But for me, 'being with' is the most significant, for a few reasons. The first is because I think it's how God relates to us. The second is that I think it's the way Jesus' ministry works. The third is that I think it anticipates heaven – when there'll be nothing left to fix, and we'll actually have to spend the time being with one another, with God, with renewed creation and with ourselves.

'Being with' is different from 'working with', because the 'working with' approach would still suggest that the most significant thing about a person experiencing homelessness is that they are homeless. By contrast, the 'being with' approach seeks to know someone as a person: their likes, dislikes, skills, talents, life story. It acknowledges that even if we seem to be someone who has all the assets (such as a house, disposable income, a stable family), we still need to experience the restoration of Christ in our relationships with others – and in our attitudes towards those very same assets.

As I (Rich) have mentioned already, in my twenties I lived in London and worked in the civil service. At one point, I was working on some important international negotiations. I felt, 'I've made it – this is changing the world!' (It makes me laugh, thinking back now!) One day, I was rushing home through Victoria station and I felt God prompt me to stop and talk to a homeless person sitting near the entrance. On this occasion I managed to follow the prompting and stop, and we had a brief conversation. Nothing remarkable happened, no lightning conversion, no obvious breakthrough. Just a conversation between two human beings, for five minutes, outside the station. But as I walked away, I felt God say: 'That conversation was the most significant thing you did for my kingdom today.' It was 'being with'.

One of the regular contributors to our Praxis Labs course is Rachel Medina, Head of Operations at the Snowdrop Project.[1] Snowdrop provides long-term holistic support, empowering survivors of human trafficking to recover from their past and rebuild their future. In their training for their case workers, they discuss a psychotherapy concept called the 'drama triangle' (see Fig. 4).[2] These are roles that people occupy in oppressive situations, but they can also

Handling power

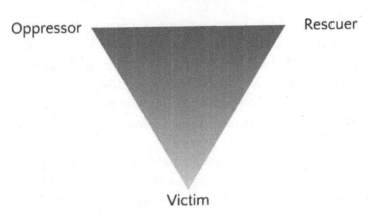

Oppressor   Rescuer

Victim

Figure 4 **The drama triangle**

describe how we choose to behave in situations where oppression has ceased or diminished. When we do this, as soon as one person assumes one of the roles in the triangle, it creates pressure for others to inhabit the other roles.

For example, we've probably all found ourselves playing the victim at some point in our lives: feeling that nothing we do can change our situation, and bemoaning our hopelessness to others. This behaviour invites a rescuer; it creates emotional pressure for someone to come and fix things for us. Conversely, I'm sure we've all been in conversations where we share a problem, simply looking for a knowing nod or some solidarity, when instead someone feels compelled to offer solution after solution; they play the rescuer, pushing us into the 'victim' role. (We often kick back against this, because we don't want a victim–rescuer transaction.)

The drama triangle is a useful diagram for us because, in activism situations, people often slip into 'rescuer mode'.

But doing this puts pressure on the person you are trying to support, pushing them to remain in the victim role. The truth is that *none* of the roles on the diagram corresponds to a true identity for one of God's people.

Now, we would all accept that no one is called to be a victim or an oppressor. But we might get a bit more uncomfortable with the idea that we're not called to be a rescuer. Why would that not be a suitable role? We can draw a parallel between the rescuer role and 'working for'. When taking on the role, we assume that we can make better decisions than another person, and, even with the best intentions, we exert power over them. Is that helping them to find their voice or to become all that God intended them to be (in the words that Thobes used at the start of this chapter)? Is it a role that we can truly say, hand on heart, God wants us to play?

Having said this, it is worth noting that in times of acute crisis a rescuer (such as a paramedic, police officer or firefighter) is definitely needed, and it may be that you are called to one of these roles. However, this is the exception to the rule. Once the acute crisis has passed, it is important that people are supported to make their own choices and have influence over their own lives, rather than being kept in a victim space.

The rescuer role can come very close to playing God in the lives of others. Two leading international development practitioners, Jayakumar Christian and Bryant Myers, have examined this idea in the context of poverty: when we play God in the lives of other people, we have stopped being who we are meant to be.[3] And losing sight of our true identity also leads us to misread our true vocation in the world. Part of the point here is that the liberation of the rich (in the above example of Jayakumar and Bryant) is in some ways bound up with the liberation of the poor, even if the rich don't see it this way or even recognise their need for liberation.

The better way for everyone is to leave the drama triangle behind, instead walking alongside people, supporting them to make their own choices about their lives and recognising that we have something to learn on the journey too.

Through her experience of 'being with' people over the years, Thobes has seen God bring transformation. The deepest form of poverty is a broken sense of identity: not seeing yourself as fully human, thinking you have nothing to give. When this is healed, it's an incredible thing. She shared a beautiful picture of what it can look like:

> If you can tap into the gold that God has put inside you; if you are able to push through the crap that life has thrown at you to take your space in society, in your community, participating in it and shaping it – bringing the change that you are passionate about . . . When someone finds the thing that fuels them and energises them to hope, and runs with it, I get excited.

This is what we want for everyone.

But how does 'being with' work when applied to huge, systemic things, such as the climate crisis? Surely, that's all about 'working for'? When we asked Sam about this recently, he explained it not with an example about the climate but like this:

If you give what you might call the definitive 'being with' example, which is sitting by the bedside of a dying person, there's nothing you can really do. You can't stop them dying, but you're determined to show God's love to them by your constancy. However, there is sometimes something you can do: you can go and get them a drink of water; you can go and fetch the nurse; you can help them with the bathroom. You actually can do some things. It would be absurd to say that helping a dying person go to the bathroom is 'working with' rather than 'being with'. The idea that you'd say 'I can't help you go to the bathroom, because my job is to sit here and hold your hand' is obviously absurd.

So, in the same way, there are some ways in which 'being with' naturally issues elements of 'working with' and even 'working for'. 'Being with' is the purpose and the goal, but it's not always the only means.

What a helpful way of thinking about it! 'Being with' should be the ultimate aim of all our activism, but it can still express itself in other ways at appropriate points. This harks back to one of our foundations for activism in chapter 1: the primacy of love. And it also connects with the idea of shalom that we looked at in chapter 2. Sam goes on:

I don't really see shalom and 'being with' as significantly different. Christ has come to be the embodiment of shalom. And sometimes that involves healings, sometimes that involves confrontation with authorities. We could see it as, 'Because of my "being with" the Father, or because of my "being with" the poor, I find myself in confrontation with the authorities. I find myself in confrontation with the authorities because they are not with the programme. That programme is the shalom of my being with the Father and being with the poor.' It's a teleological structure, by which you may have to leave the bedside to go and get a drink of water, but it's all for the sake of being with the dying person.

We should be modelling this 'being with' in our lives (and if we do so, we'll find ourselves rather less likely to burn out, as we'll discover in chapter 9!). Our activism should flow from it, and be as consistent with this concept as possible, bearing in mind that it will be necessary at times to do things that look more like 'working with' (or even 'working for').

When we've talked about this in the past, people quite often say: 'That sounds great, but how does "being with" work for climate activism? Or many of the other big, systemic injustices that we face today?' This is an excellent question.

With the example of the climate crisis, we need to frame our action within the ultimate aim of 'being with'. It is possible for us to 'be with' our environment – to enjoy it, to delight in the creation God has given us. Children are really good at this! Jumping into puddles with welly boots on, blowing dandelion seeds off their stalks, or simply playing hide-and-seek among the trees. I (Rachel) love it when I get the opportunity to tap into that childlike joy by racing waves on the beach, or trying to find my favourite autumn leaf in the park. Creation is a good thing God has given to us, and we can worship him with and through our enjoyment of it. Being with him and being with his creation can happen at the same time.

For another example, Sam pointed us in the direction of the Pulitzer Prize-winning novel *The Overstory* by Richard Powers.[4] Without giving away too many spoilers, a key moment in the book comes when climate activists Nick and Olivia climb up into the uppermost branches of a huge redwood tree to prevent it from being cut down by commercial loggers. The activists end up spending months, rather than days, up the tree, making a clear statement: 'If the tree goes, I go too.' What an example of 'being with'! 'Being with' doesn't have to be as explicit as this, but it should frame our activism.

Let's talk a bit more about how this all works in practice. Whole books have been written about this, but here we will suggest three simple keys. These aren't formulas; they are more like parables or questions that we keep returning to, and try to live our way into.

We already have the first: that **the idea of 'being with' should be the overall aim and purpose of our activism.** At its heart, our activism is about joining in with God's work of mending broken relationships. Everything should flow from this. Think of a church soup kitchen. It's busy; there are people getting food from the counter and sitting down at tables to eat. In the kitchen, people experiencing homelessness and people with a steady home are cooking together. It's lively and bustling, and everyone is getting a much-needed hot meal. But more important than this, even, is that all the people there get a chance to stop bustling: to sit, be, chat and eat together. The deepest purpose of the project is to create space for 'being with' – to allow true, authentic relationships to develop and reconciliation to happen. This often happens over food!

The second is to recognise that **we need to seek as close an alignment as possible between our ends and our means**. As Sam put it, 'Your activism, ideally, should be demonstrating the good that you are propounding so that nobody can be mistaken about what it is really about.' There's no doubt that the most inspiring activists take this approach. The well-known climate activist Greta Thunberg is a fantastic example of this: she doesn't use air travel, she doesn't buy new clothes (only second-hand if absolutely necessary), she won't give interviews to anyone who has flown to see her, and she donates all the money she receives (apart from her student grant) to charity in order to spark conversation.[5] Her message – that we desperately need to do something to address climate change, *now* – is backed up by the way she lives her life.

In the case of systemic injustice, a big part of this alignment between ends and means comes through recognising that we are caught up in the system we want to fight, and taking action to change this. For example, in the case of climate change, we know that lots of our activities generate carbon emissions. So, we can choose options that generate less carbon dioxide (CO_2), such as buying less red meat and dairy, using public transport, and cycling or walking to work – and we can contact our local decision-makers, asking them to improve public transport services and the cycle network in our area. Alternatively, we could take a leaf out of Greta's book and only buy or source second-hand goods, or drastically limit our purchases of new items.

In the case of injustices such as sexism, racism, ableism and others, we are also caught up in the systems that we want to fight. It's a reality that, as a white straight man, I (Rich) benefit – sometimes without even realising it – from the way the world works. This is true for many of us, on many levels. For our Praxis Labs course, we developed an exercise to help explain what I mean by this, and we've included a version of it below.

Exercise: 'Privileges for sale'. Imagine you have £1,800. Look through the list of twenty-four attributes in Table 2. Which would you choose to purchase? What would you go without?

(For the purpose of the exercise, no matter what experiences or identity you have, you do not have any of the privileges on the list.)

Now, imagine you have just £300. Which of the privileges would you choose to purchase then?

Before we move on to the third and final key, it might be helpful to reflect on the following:

- When doing the exercise, what questions did you wrestle with when trying to make decisions? What struck you about the list?

Table 2 Privileges for sale

Privilege	Cost
Being free to express your opinion without having people ignore you or speak over you	£100
Not being judged by how you look	£100
Being able to seek out and spend time with 'people like you' if you want to	£100
When you ask for the person in charge, finding that it's someone you can identify with	£100
Being able to understand and make yourself understood in the language of the place where you live	£100
Having free access to healthcare	£100
Being free from the expectation that some things are inappropriate for you to do	£100
Being free from fear of harassment when walking alone at night	£100
Being free from (ignorant) questions or jokes about your race/ethnicity/sex	£100
Not having to work while you attend university	£100
Being able to find plasters at mainstream stores that are designed to match your skin tone	£100
Being free from problems at immigration when crossing borders	£100
Having access to outdoor space at home (a garden or yard)	£100
Feeling the police are there to protect you, rather than suspicious of you	£100
Being told 'You can be anything you want to be' from a young age	£100
Growing up in an area that was generally regarded as safe (e.g. not known for crime, prostitution, drug activity)	£100
Never having to skip a meal for lack of money	£100
Being able to access your school, office, public transport and other spaces easily (e.g. without needing a ramp)	£100
Owning a car	£100
Not being stared at in public	£100
Having a high degree of autonomy at work, rather than being subject to micromanagement and control	£100
Having your identity and the history of people 'like you' affirmed at school	£100
Being able to speak for yourself and not have others assume they will speak for you	£100
Being able to make mistakes and not have people attribute your behaviour to flaws in your racial or gender group	£100

- How do you think differences in access to these things affect our relationships?
- How do you think awareness of our differences in access affects our activism?

***

The last key is something called 'decentring': **creating space for those who have been (or still are) the victims of injustice and oppression to take the starring role in their own story.** To put it another way, this would mean that those without a particular 'privilege' from the list in the previous exercise are at the heart of finding ways to extend access to it to others.

Remember the drama triangle from earlier in the chapter (Fig. 4)? Decentring is about leaving the triangle behind: coming alongside people to accompany and support them as we journey together. We can lend our skills and talents to the cause, but ultimately we want others with direct, lived experience of the oppression we are fighting to be the ones in the driving seat. So, it might be that an anti-trafficking charity seeks to have survivors of human trafficking on their board of trustees, or in influential positions within the charity. It might be that in discussions around the climate crisis, prominence is given to those who are already feeling the effects of the devastating changes to our environment. It might be that those who are experiencing homelessness take the lead in deciding the menu for a soup kitchen, or activities for a social night.

Doing activism in a way that's consistent with these three keys often makes things messier and more complex.

But this is also how true transformation happens. If acting out of love were straightforward, there would have been no need for Paul to write these words in 1 Corinthians 13:

> Love is patient, love is kind. It does not envy, it does not boast, it is not proud. It does not dishonour others, it is not self-seeking, it is not easily angered, it keeps no record of wrongs. Love does not delight in evil but rejoices with the truth. It always protects, always trusts, always hopes, always perseveres.[6]

And so we come back to love, and its primacy, in all our actions.

Questions for reflection

There is a lot to take in and think about in this chapter! Here are a few questions to help you process it:

- What was your initial reaction to Sam Wells's framework of 'working for / being for / working with / being with'?
- How did you feel after it had been explained with the example of the drama triangle and the link back to shalom?
- Can you see how it relates to any areas of activism that you are involved with? What do you think you need to consider changing? What might become more difficult?
- How did you find the 'privileges for sale' exercise? What insights did you gain from this? How did it make you feel?

We finished the chapter talking about three keys:

1 The idea of 'being with' should be the overall aim and purpose of our activism.
2 We need to seek as close an alignment as possible between 'our ends' and 'our means' (meaning we need integrity in activism).
3 'Decentring' is vital: creating space for those who have been (or still are) the victims of injustice and oppression to take the starring role in their own story.

Can you see how these three keys relate to forms of activism that you are involved with? How can you reflect on them further? How can you move into applying them in your own life?

Recommended resources

- Sam Wells's interview 'The Power of Being With: Relationship at the core', *Hopeful Activists* podcast, 9 August 2019
- Brian Fikkert and Steve Corbett, *When Helping Hurts: How to alleviate poverty without hurting the poor . . . and yourself*, rev. edn (Chicago, IL: Moody, 2014)
- Samuel Wells, *A Nazareth Manifesto: Being with God* (Chichester: Wiley, 2015)
- Ben Lindsay, *We Need to Talk about Race: Understanding the black experience in white majority churches* (London: SPCK, 2019)

6

Demystifying campaigning

In the previous five chapters, we've looked at some of the important principles, heart attitudes and motivations behind healthy activism. This chapter is where things start to get practical. We're going to explore what campaigning is and how to do it effectively, as well as hearing some stories of campaigns in the UK, both local and national.

I wonder what your idea of campaigning is? Maybe it's placards held up at protests, or politicians and party members out knocking on doors ahead of an election. Maybe it's provocative theatre, or people typing out emails to their MP. Maybe it's knitted art installations on piers, even! We've sought out the wisdom of experienced Tearfund campaigner Jack Wakefield and young climate activist Christine Meyer to help us think it through.

But first, a question for reflection before we get into the nitty-gritty: **When was the last time someone changed your mind about something? What was it that convinced you?**

***

If, like me (Rachel), you have struggled to get your head around exactly what campaigning is, Jack has a very helpful definition: 'Campaigning is influencing the actions of those in power to bring about justice.' 'Those in power' could be people in the community, church leaders, politicians, business leaders and corporations, those involved in global decision-making processes . . . whoever holds sway. Campaigning is working to influence them so that they change their actions to bring about justice.

Let's start by looking at an example of campaigning from the Bible. Jack pointed us to the book of Esther: she's a good campaigner, and so is her cousin Mordecai. Near the start of the narrative, Mordecai hears of a plot to wipe out all of God's people. Understandably, he's horrified by it and wants to do whatever he can to stop it. So he sends a series of messages to his relative, Esther, who at this point has become queen and lives in the palace of the Persian king, Xerxes.

Mordecai lobbies Esther, in effect: he tells her she has the power and capability to make a difference. She does listen to him (after some rather dramatic tactics on Mordecai's part) and considers what he has to say. In Esther chapter 4, we see her response:

> Go, gather together all the Jews who are in Susa, and fast for me. Do not eat or drink for three days, night or day. I and my attendants will fast as you do. When this is done, I will go to the king, even though it is against the law. And if I perish, I perish.[1]

What a significant thing to say! Esther is taking a huge risk by going and speaking to the king about the injustice. It was forbidden to approach the king without being summoned, and he could have her put to death for doing it, but she knew she had to speak up.

Jack pointed us in the direction of five helpful questions that all campaigners must ask themselves. Three are based on thinking from Kirsty McNeill at Save the Children,[2] and Jack has added the last two. For now, we're going to consider the first two of these questions.

Key campaign question 1: What do you want?

For Mordecai, the answer is pretty straightforward: for his people not to be wiped out in a few months' time, as per the royal edict that had been issued. This might seem quite different from the sort of 'asks' we have today! However, if you reflect for a moment, it's actually not too different from the asks we might have to do with climate change or humanitarian crises.

On the *Hopeful Activists* podcast, we've heard examples of students wanting their university to create scholarships for those severely affected by political or humanitarian crises; a local community wanting to stop the opening of a new opencast coal mine; and activists wanting a government to uphold its ban on thin plastics (among others).[3] Other examples might include convincing a church leader to take action on climate change, or asking a local councillor to provide the necessary permissions for a community café.

Nailing down what you want – having a clear 'ask' – is key to making a campaign successful. If you're working on a campaign right now, what is it that you want? Can you sum it up in one sentence?

Key campaign question 2: Who can give it to you?

For Mordecai, the person who could stop the genocide was King Xerxes. And Mordecai also knew one person with access to the king: his cousin Esther. He needed to influence her in order to be able to influence the king. In the examples from the podcast, the people in a position to meet the demands of campaigners were university authorities and those with the funds to be able to support scholarships: the local government and the national government.

We'll return to Esther's story, and some of the stories from the podcast, later in this chapter.

For now, let's consider another campaign example. There aren't many bigger asks in the world at the moment than stopping climate change! We asked Jack about how, through his role with Tearfund, he'd been involved in campaigning around the climate crisis, and this is what he shared:

In 2021, I was part of a youth campaign, called Take a Stand, around climate change ahead of the G7[4] and COP26[5], supporting young Christians to have their voices heard. Before the G7 Summit, we worked with the young people to draft a letter to world leaders, and crowdsourced translations of the letter into the languages of the world leaders who were coming. We also worked with the local MP to see if we could get the letter into the welcome packs of the world leaders.

We considered what stunts we could do: we did a prayer walk with local politicians past the venues where leaders were negotiating, and we chalked on the roads the name of the campaign. At one point we were being followed around by the street cleaners; they wanted it to look beautiful, and we were there chalking everything! We organised media interviews for the young people and put together a film of them all reading the letter – that kind of thing.

The campaign was gaining attention and momentum, but **what did they want?**

We wanted world leaders to *do something* about climate change, but it needed to be more specific. You need a clear target when campaigning, and that was one of the things we found challenging. Ultimately, the young people's asks were for world leaders to fund adaptation money for people who are already impacted by climate change, and to commit to not funding fossil fuel projects overseas any more.

So that was Take a Stand's ask, and Jack has also already indicated **who could give this to them:** world leaders. But world leaders don't exist in a vacuum! They are influenced by their ministers, civil servants, friends, spouses and many other people. Just as Mordecai had to turn to Esther to find a way of influencing King Xerxes, our route to people in power will also often be a meandering one. And this is where a favourite tool of campaigners comes in handy: the power map (see Fig. 5).

This map is a grid you can use in order to think through who is supportive of your cause (towards the right of the grid) and who has the influence to be able to change things (towards the top). The process can also help you figure out who might be in a position to deny your ask (those in the top-left quadrant). You don't have to have a personal connection to everyone on your power map! Start by putting anyone on there who you think could have an effect on the outcome of your campaign, and estimating where they might be on the grid.

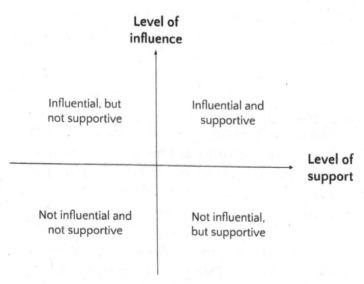

Figure 5 A blank power map

Once you have the power map filled in, you can start to get an idea of how your campaign needs to take shape. Your aim is to try to move people to the right along the grid so that they become more supportive. (Alternatively, if someone is in staunch opposition to your cause, you might attempt to move them down the grid, so that their influence is less strongly felt.)

Let's take a relatively simple example: influencing a church leader to take action on climate change. In this hypothetical case (which may not be too far removed from reality for some!), a member of the congregation – let's call her Julie – would like to see her church take steps to address its energy consumption and move towards more renewable sources. Her ask is for the church to install solar panels on the roof of the church building, which would reduce the church's reliance on fossil fuels. Her friends in her home group are very supportive, though when she mentioned the idea to the church treasurer, he wasn't keen on the idea because of the cost of the installation. Julie's vicar is more ambivalent about the matter but is concerned about how they would approach the faculties board of the Church of England for planning permission. The church's youth worker is more supportive and has an idea to involve the young people in the church in raising funds for the panels.

Julie's power map would look a bit like Figure 6. If you want, you could have a go at drawing up a power map now. Pick an issue that you're working on locally (perhaps even in your own church), and jot down the key groups and people on a chart like the one we've provided as a sample.

After drawing up your power map, you might look at it

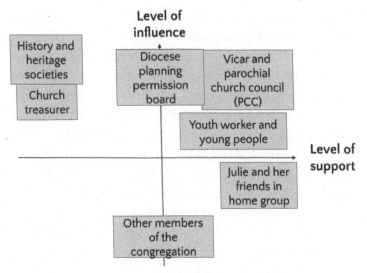

Figure 6 A sample filled-in power map

and think, 'But I have no way of influencing any of these people!' This is a very understandable feeling! However, you may find that there are more possibilities than you think. We'll explain why as we consider the next three questions that all campaigners should consider.

Question 3 is a big one: why should the people in positions of influence do what you want? Or as Kirsty McNeill (Advocacy Director at Save the Children) likes to say: 'Why haven't they given it to me already?'

Key campaign question 3: Why haven't they given it to you already?

Some people have an uncanny knack for knowing intuitively what the answer to this question is, and therefore how to proceed. My (Rich's) 7-year-old son, Aidan, is one of those people. If he asks for an ice cream and I say 'No', he always seems to have a sense of what will get him that ice cream. Sometimes, that might mean mobilising other powerful constituencies (maybe his brother) or involving another person on his intuitive 'power map', such as his mum. At other times, he simply asks me again, really politely with a big smile. Once, he led his friends in the chant: '*What do we want?*' 'Ice cream!' '*When do we want it?*' 'Now!' (At least he was listening at those climate protests!) It helps to have one of these powerful people on your team, but let's also be a little systematic and think through some of the potential answers to question 3:

- Perhaps the decision-makers simply don't realise that there's a problem, or don't know about your solution. Or perhaps they don't agree with you about it!
- Alternatively, they may agree with you, but simply have little incentive to act. Other issues could be crowding you out; after all, many decision-makers have very limited amounts of time and resources and have to choose how to spend them.
- And, of course, it may also be true that the opposing side is more powerful than you. If you're going up against a big corporation (say, trying to prevent the opening of a new coal mine, as in one of the examples from the *Hopeful Activists* podcast), then this will be a serious consideration.[6]

The key thing to recognise here is that the way you answer this question will help determine the approach that you pursue. When Aidan asked me for an ice cream, maybe I said he couldn't have one simply because my attention was on something else – in which case, his chant was a pretty effective way to get my attention! Or let's look at the example we mentioned above: the local community trying to stop development of a new opencast coal mine. Here, campaigners sought to tip the scales by mobilising powerful voices (to counter the powerful vested interests they were facing), such as Sir David Attenborough and the international campaign group Friends of the Earth. Their involvement (and the publicity generated by it) helped to persuade the UK government to deny planning permission for the mine.[7]

Think back to your answer to the reflection question at the start of the chapter. **How was it that your mind was changed? And why had it not been changed before?** Take some time to pause and think this through, writing down notes on a piece of paper or in your journal if that's helpful.

***

In some campaigns, there may be several answers to the question of why the people with influence haven't given you your ask already, and therefore there may be several obstacles to success. A few years ago, I (Rich) was part of a team trying to launch a community café on the edge of a neglected park in Bradford, and there were certainly several obstacles in our path! They neatly illustrate how your tactics need to match your answer to key question 3, so let's go through them.

- Initially, the members of the city council were sceptical that the café would ever become commercially viable. So they said no to giving us a peppercorn (very cheap) lease on the old park lodge that we needed. **This was barrier 1.** With a genuine intellectual disagreement like this, it seemed better to try to convince them with facts and figures, rather than protesting by marching through the streets. We went away and wrote up a detailed business case with lots of research, figures and projections. And it worked! The council agreed to give us the building, on the proviso that we could raise the money needed to renovate it.

- Fast-forward a year (skimming over a lot of work!), and the money had been promised by two grant-giving bodies and an impact investment group. However, to release the cash, the funders wanted to see a signed lease agreement with the council. And the council's legal department wasn't sending the paperwork. With the deadline set by the funders drawing near, we were facing **barrier 2**: other priorities in the legal department were crowding out our need for the paperwork.

  At the time, I thought it was crazy that we might miss out on the chance to create a community hub – despite having convinced the council and raised a shedload of cash – just because the council's lawyers were busy. But honestly, this is *exactly* why campaigning is so important. It was time to make some noise!

But how were we to do so effectively? We did some power mapping, and realised that our local councillor was the deputy council leader. All local councillors hold regular 'surgeries' where local people can come and raise their issues, so we also had a way of getting to him. We decided to turn up at one of his surgeries en masse. In my experience, only a couple of people normally attend these surgeries, so when a group of people turned up, bedecked in the orange hoodies of the local community group, it was clear that he had a problem. He pulled out his phone and sent a message to someone, and the next day I received an email from a senior council official: 'This community café has now become a political issue – tell me what you need.'

It still makes me smile remembering that victory, although it felt very stressful at the time! Working on a campaign at any level can be a real rollercoaster of emotion, but there's also often a fair bit of drudgery in the meetings and 'admin'.

We've heard from Jack about the climate campaign; now let's hear from one of the young people who was involved. This is how Christine described what it was like to be part of the campaign:

Within Take a Stand, a core group of young Christians from around the UK would get together to discuss how our campaigning was going. I hadn't seen many of the people in person, but we had a group chat where we messaged one another, and we met up on a video call every three weeks; it created quite a cool community, even though many of us hadn't seen each other in real life. It shows how technology can help. We still managed to build this campaign despite never seeing each other! I live in quite a small village, so it was a really good experience to see so many other young Christians passionate about these justice issues.

Each of us in the core team spoke to our MPs about the campaign, and we each tried to get fifty people in our church or community to sign the Take a Stand open letter – to raise awareness and get it out there as much as possible. From that, the campaign grew. Some of us even spoke to the archbishop of Canterbury in the run-up to COP26.

What was really cool was that not all forty of us did everything. We divided up the different tasks or ideas that we had, because people had different skills or time commitments. That meant that we could achieve way more than if one person had done it all, or if we were all trying to do everything. So some people went and spoke to the archbishop of Canterbury, some people managed to get some fundraising for our campaign, some people spoke to news reporters . . . There were lots of little roles, so everyone was able to use their skills to the best benefit of the campaign. I wrote a document so that people knew how to speak to their MPs, as lots of people may not have done that before.

For Jack and Christine, there were two further questions that had a big bearing on the tactics that they chose. The first of these is to do with your target person.

Key campaign question 4:
What does the person you are targeting care about?

To address question 4, the young people pooled their knowledge. Jack describes their approach:

> We knew that the local MP in Cornwall really cared about young people's engagement, and so we had an 'in' there. We knew, too, that he was good friends with the prime minister, who was one of the G7 leaders. We also knew that the world leaders were talking about climate change – it was going to be on the agenda of their meetings. We knew there would be some receptiveness but didn't think that they would talk about the specific asks we had, so we tried to lead into them gradually.

To think through the perspectives of the G7 leaders and the local MP, Jack and the team used the principles behind one of the activities in the Difference course (run by the archbishop of Canterbury's Reconciliation Ministry; there's a link to it at the end of this chapter). In the activity, three chairs are set out in a row (see Fig. 7). When you sit in the first chair, you share your perspective on an issue: what you think should happen, and why you

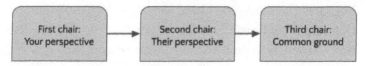

Figure 7 The 'three chairs' activity

think it. Then you move to the second chair and try to articulate what the other person's view is: how and why they don't agree with you (and, perhaps, why their ideas might have merit). And then, moving to the third chair, you try to find areas of common ground – the places where compromise is possible, or where your arguments connect.

Jack and the team used these ideas to find the common ground between their ask and the G7 leaders' perspective. Then, to hone their tactics, they thought about the next big question.

Key campaign question 5:
What do you already have?

Jack shares:

We didn't have a big budget. It was a team of young people and a couple of us supporting them. We didn't have loads of time – we started the campaign a month or so before the G7 Summit. But what we did have was lots of young people in the local area, who were part of churches and schools that were full of loads more people.

When it comes to this final question, there's another tool that can be useful: the network map. This is different from the power map! After you have identified the decision-makers using the power map, the network map will help you think through how you can approach and influence them.

Take a large sheet of paper and start by writing your name in the centre, and the decision-makers at the edge. Add in the groups and people you are connected to, and the groups and people the decision-makers are connected to. Do any of those connections have links to one another? Keep going with the map until you have established links from you to the decision-makers. Think about which people on the map can help you influence the key decision-makers directly or by helping to grow the campaign. In Figure 8 you can see a sample map from the Take a Stand campaign.

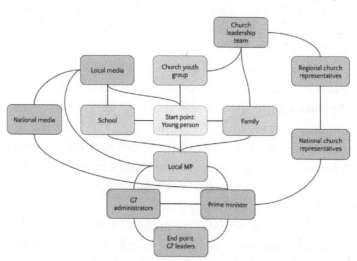

Figure 8 A sample network map from the Take a Stand campaign before the G7 Summit in 2021

Jack continues:

The young people were doing stuff in their schools, they were talking to local media, they met their MP . . . If we wanted to influence the prime minister, these young people in Cornwall and us Tearfund staff didn't have that direct link to him. But what we could do was contact the local MP, who was then able to brief the prime minister *and* talk about it at Number 10 Downing Street before the G7 happened. So within a few weeks of us launching the campaign, it was talked about at Number 10, because we thought through what we already had available to us.

Let's return to Esther's story. When we left her, she, Mordecai and the Jewish people were praying and fasting for three days before she took the risk of approaching the king (campaigning often requires guts, and Esther clearly had this in abundance). Interestingly, after those three days, she didn't go to him to talk about the genocide. Instead, she initially asked him to attend a series of banquets. It's an intriguing tactic. Part of me wonders if Esther might have been praying and reflecting about a similar question: 'What does the king care about?' And maybe Xerxes really cared about food and banquets!

Having experienced the banquets and Esther's hospitality, Xerxes became amenable to her request to revoke the royal edict calling for the genocide. He issued a new edict, giving the Jewish people the right to defend themselves against attack, and honoured Esther and Mordecai. Their campaign was successful.

***

So, we've looked through the five key questions that all campaigners must answer:

- **What do you want?**
- **Who can give it to you?**
- **Why haven't they given it to you already?**
- **What does the person you are targeting care about?**
- **What do you already have?**

They're invaluable, but they're not a formula. Sometimes you'll have a neat campaign all planned out using these questions and tools, and it will come to nothing. At other times you'll make it up as you go along and it will work fantastically. In fact, being prepared to make it up as we go along, with a bit of prayer, is probably one of the most useful skills we can learn in campaigning!

Christine's story of how her local community embraced and ran with her litter-picking campaign illustrates this, and also shows how campaigning can overlap with local projects (the subject of the next chapter). She shares:

In early 2021, I did Tearfund's Emerging Influencers course for young people, and during it, we had to do a fundraising task. I decided to do a number of litter picks throughout March, and I got other people involved. I spoke about it at my church and in my community,

95

and that inspired others to start something long-term. It's incredible how passionate our church has become about these issues; it's grown way bigger than I thought it would have, and it's nothing that I really did. We have book swaps so people don't have to buy books, and plant swaps so we can get new plants. Our church now has a big focus on climate change – it's mentioned in our prayers every week. And it does influence the council and our MPs: a bike lane is being built around here now. I'm about to leave the village to go to university, but others have picked it up and it will continue once I've left the village. It shows that you just need one person to put out a little spark, to inspire others, and then they'll do it.

Christine's faith in God also grew and developed over the course of her campaign:

I think before doing Emerging Influencers, I didn't really connect climate justice much to God. But now I see that by protecting his creation I am loving God and loving my neighbours. I have really seen God through the work of this, just because of how quickly it grew – surely God is working there. All these opportunities came to us, just at the right time.

Honestly, in our experience, this is often how God works. Things can sometimes come together organically, without our meticulous planning – but with prayer, and by the power of the Holy Spirit.

This leads us on to the last, most significant part of campaigning. In the hustle and bustle, it can be easy to forget to pray. But Jack has seen first-hand how prayer can make all the difference to the outcome of a campaign:

We've really seen prayer turn things around. We'd been campaigning for years at Tearfund about the billions of pounds that the UK government spends on funding fossil fuel projects in other countries – we wanted that money to be moved into renewables. We have a community of people who pray with us, and in 2020 we heard that the subject was being talked about at Downing Street. So we messaged them to ask them to pray.

Then it all went quiet; the conversations ended and nothing came of it. We had been campaigning in coalition with lots of other organisations, and they were beginning to say, 'Oh well, let's try again next year.' But we sent another message out, asking our community to pray that we would see some change. A week later, we heard that the conversation had started again in Downing Street.

So we messaged everyone, letting them know that the conversation had started again and asking them to keep praying. Two weeks after that message, the prime minister announced that the UK would be the first major economy to stop funding fossil fuel projects in other countries. It was literally three weeks from feeling like we'd lost the campaign to then seeing this amazing turnaround: an announcement in public of exactly what we were wanting.

It was an encouragement to me that prayer has a massive role in campaigning – in dramatic ways like that, and also in guiding our decision-making, helping us think through our tactics. Prayer is crucial for us to hold our campaigns in context as well. It would be easy to feel like we have to solve it all ourselves, that it's on our shoulders, that if we don't win our campaign then it's our fault that the injustice is still there. But when we're praying regularly and giving everything to God, then we're reminded that our job isn't to be super-successful. It's not even to win our campaigns! Our job as followers of Jesus is to be faithful to him, to honour him with all of our lives and all of our energy, not forgetting that he is the one who creates, sustains and redeems the world.

There's a brilliant Christian Extinction Rebellion activist who said to me that the call on us as Christians is to be faithful, not necessarily successful. We are invited to join in with Jesus, but the invitation is to faithfulness, not necessarily to success. Praying about our campaigning helps us to remember that, and to not carry the whole burden ourselves.

Let's close with a final reflection from Jack on the book of Esther:

One thing I quite like about the book of Esther is that God isn't mentioned in the book. I think that's helpful for us as campaigners, because often when you're looking injustice in the face, you can feel despair.

'Where is God in all of this? This is so bad, the world is so broken – where is God?'

But when you read the book of Esther it's obvious that God has got his hand on the whole story. He facilitates the whole thing. He prepares Mordecai and Esther, he protects them in their conversations, he brings about change in the end . . . but he's not mentioned in it. I think it's a reminder to us that when we look back, we can see God all over stuff. In the moment, when we're looking at injustice, it can be really hard to see him, but it doesn't mean he's not there.

Questions for reflection

If you are thinking about starting or joining a campaign:

- What do you want?
- Who can give it to you?
- Why haven't they given it to you already?
- What do they care about?
- What do you already have?

Recommended resources

- 'Campaign Successes: Starting something new' episode, *Hopeful Activists* podcast, 18 November 2020: praxiscentre.org/podcast-archives/ campaign-successes-starting-something-new
- Tearfund's advocacy toolkit: learn.tearfund. org/en/resources/series/roots-guides/ advocacy-toolkit--a-roots-guide

- Kirsty McNeill's article on 'the questions campaigners hate to answer, but need to': www.bond.org.uk/news/2019/01/question-campaigners-hate-to-answer
- *Pride*, the 2014 film about lesbian and gay activists who supported the Welsh miners' strikes
- The Influencing course from Christians in Politics: influencecourse.co.uk
- The Difference course: difference.rln.global
- Sarah Corbett, *How to Be a Craftivist: The art of gentle protest* (London: Unbound, 2017)

7

Going local

There are *so* many different forms of activism – almost as many as there are activists – that we could never cover them all in this book. However, we want to give you a flavour of two groups of approaches that are relevant to lots of different situations. We covered campaigning in the previous chapter, and in this chapter we'll look at the second approach: developing local projects that address specific needs. (As we'll see, the two often end up connecting to each other.) We will also touch on a third that is even closer to home: showing hospitality. (If we had space for a fourth approach, it would probably be something to do with the arts. After all, beauty and creativity are important in their own right as expressions of shalom.)

When we think of local projects, we often think of needs that scream out to us – where a clear and urgent response is required. At the time we're writing this, in the winter of 2022/2023, one of these is the cost-of-living crisis. Community kitchens, food banks, warm spaces and various other local projects have been expanded and created to try to respond to the injustice and suffering around us. In summer 2022, the refugee crisis was another urgent need, with large numbers of people relocating to the UK from Ukraine, Afghanistan and Hong Kong.

How do we respond effectively to needs like these?

A helpful framework for thinking about this is the **project management cycle**, and we're going to take a whistle-stop tour of this in a minute (we'll make it more interesting than it sounds!). Setting up projects that respond to a specific (often immediate) need is a vital way of living out our call to follow Jesus' path of love, but what has got us really excited as we've researched this chapter is how these projects – when they have a strong emphasis on 'being with' – result in fertile ground for going further than the immediate need: they can also lay the foundations for addressing systemic injustices.

We spoke to Hannah Ling, Social Justice Advisor in the diocese of Oxford, who told us about a project near Reading that illustrates this. Over the past few years, lots of people have fled Hong Kong and settled near Reading, because it's a tech hub and lots of them have previous careers in IT. The group started off with a pretty standard approach, which met an immediate need: they provided English classes for new arrivals. This was important in its own right, but it also provided a foundation for further action. Hannah shared:

> We realised that people were applying for jobs that they had the qualifications for, but they weren't getting them – or even interviews sometimes. We wondered why that was! So we gathered some of the people who were in the English classes to do some action: we went outside three key headquarters in Reading to ask to speak with the HR team about why people weren't getting the jobs. We wanted to know what the barriers were and ask if the companies wanted to support

Hong Kongers and other migrant groups to get access to the jobs that they could definitely do.

Pretty cool, huh? The initial project was important in itself (helping new arrivals to the UK learn English and find community), but it also provided a space to work together to identify and then address other, deeper challenges that the group were facing.

Before we talk more about this, let's talk project management cycles (see Fig. 9).

Identifying a need

All projects start with identifying a need. Sometimes this is obvious. To take Hannah's example above, it's clear

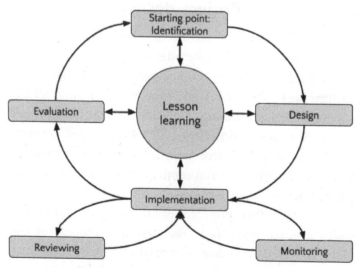

Figure 9 The project management cycle

that for many migrants and refugees, English classes are a vital stepping stone when they first arrive in the UK. In other cases, some more research and listening might be required. A couple of years ago, we spoke to Lara Bundock and Rachel Medina about the start of the Snowdrop Project, which supports survivors of human trafficking.[1] Lara had been working as a social worker in a safe house for survivors, but she realised that support for survivors simply dropped off a cliff as soon as people left the safe house after the legally prescribed period of thirty days (it used to be forty-five). Often, identifying need will relate closely to that question we considered in chapter 4 – what's God giving you hope for? – as well as listening to those you think are affected and others in your area.

Project design

Once you've identified the need, there's the question of project design. In Lara's case, after seeing the consequences of the support cliff-edge for survivors she had personally worked with, she spent some time brainstorming all the support that someone would need when they exited a safe house. She then brainstormed all the skills and training that someone would need in order to support a survivor towards independence and reintegration. That formed the basis of her initial project idea.

Sometimes this project design phase is slow, and sometimes it's really fast. The first ever episode of the *Hopeful Activists* podcast covered the story of Street Angels, who look out for those who are or could become vulnerable on nights out in clubs and pubs.[2] This went from initial idea to implementation in less than two weeks: Paul Blakey had walked around Halifax at night and seen how bad things were getting (national media were coming to film the 'wild west of Yorkshire'), and his initial idea was to open the existing Churches Together and YMCA café as a safe space in the evenings. He spoke to Churches Together and the police, and both were supportive, so they went for it.

In many cases, there are models you can learn from and even copy, but it's also worth tailoring the project to meet the specific needs of your community. For example, food banks are one way of helping to provide access to essentials; it's an established model that you can copy if you want to help people at crisis point. An alternative would be a community grocery store, where people can choose a set number of items they need for a set price (Abi Thomas, who produces the *Hopeful Activists* podcast, helps out at a Grub Club at her church in Bradford, which offers sixteen items of fruit, vegetables and staples for £5). So what does your community actually need? A food bank would probably be easier to establish, but something like the Grub Club allows people to choose what they would like and have more authority and control over their own lives.

At this stage, you'll also want to get a sense of the resources that you need, in terms of both volunteer hours, money[3] and gifts in kind (we cover the topic of team in the next chapter). At a very basic level, decisions like when to open and where to base yourselves are crucial.

In the Street Angels example above, the answers to these were pretty obvious. In other cases, the questions might need more thought. To think through how to set up the project supporting survivors of human trafficking, Lara and Rachel got a copy of the textbook *Business Planning for Dummies* and worked through the first couple of chapters together!

Implementation

Of course, there comes a point where you simply need to get on with things and learn as you go (or at least run a pilot to test the idea). When Paul Blakey turned up at the Churches Together and YMCA café on the first evening of their new venture, around fifty volunteers showed up – too many to fit into the café! So they went out onto the streets to support people where they found them, and Street Angels was born. It was only by starting out that they found the transformational model which has made such a difference to so many communities around the world.

Things aren't always as clear-cut as this. It might take a while to find the resources and space you need, or it might be that your initial plans need to change after they don't go the way you envisaged. That's fine! It's good to take steps of faith and learn as you go. The journey is rarely straightforward, and we often have to pivot and find new approaches. When Alison – whose story we'll hear more of in chapter 10 – first started setting up a community fridge in her local area, she put a lot of effort into securing some space free of charge in the local shopping centre, only to find out a few weeks later that the whole place had been sold for redevelopment! Having the tenacity to keep going and keep pivoting is key.

Reviewing, monitoring and evaluating

There are loads of great tools out there to help with the nitty-gritty of planning and running a project – business manuals and Gantt charts, budget spreadsheets and templates for team meetings, and much more – but perhaps the most important part of the diagram is also the bit that is most frequently overlooked: reviewing, monitoring and evaluating. Once a project starts, we often get so busy 'keeping the show on the road' that we forget to assess our progress and learn from our mistakes.

It's probably when a project seems to be ticking along nicely that we are most likely to overlook the need for monitoring and learning. If it isn't being forced on us by near-failure or great success, it can feel like an optional extra (if you already run some sort of project and you're reading this, I bet you know what we mean!). But if you take the core team away for a few hours to talk about how things are going – to review what is working well and what is causing the most stress – it can make a huge difference.

Recently, I (Rich) revisited the original vision for a project I'm involved with, and I was surprised to see that we were focusing much more on one element of the vision than the others. I'd even forgotten about the other elements if I'm honest! Perhaps you have a team member who is fond of asking challenging questions – uncomfortable at the time but, ultimately, hugely valuable if given time and space. Or perhaps – like me – you're not that great at taking time to celebrate when things are going well! Reviewing your progress is a great opportunity to pause and appreciate how far you have come.

Just as important as discussing these things as a team is speaking to those you seek to serve and asking them what they think. This links back to the 'three keys' we discussed at the end of chapter 5 ((1) the idea of 'being with' as the overall aim and purpose of our activism; (2) integrity in our activism – aligning 'our means' and 'our ends'; (3) 'decentring' to create space for the victims of injustice or oppression to take the starring role in their own story). These are great in theory, but in practice they are hard to crack – like questions we have to live our way into, returning to them again and again.

That's our whistle-stop tour of the project management cycle, so here are a couple of questions to help you start applying it in your context:

- Revisit what came up for you in the 'What is God giving you hope for?' exercise in chapter 4. Did this relate to key needs in your community? Write a bit more about what these needs are, and note down any ideas you might have about how you could address them. Are there any other organisations or groups near you who are already working in this area?
- If you are already involved in a local project, how is it going? What are the things that are working well, and

what is causing stress? Have you spoken to the people you're seeking to serve about how they think it's going? Why not make time to chat and hear feedback in the coming week?

The project management cycle helps us get projects off the ground more quickly and more effectively than we otherwise would. It's well worth looking at on a regular basis. However, there are also risks that we need to be aware of in taking a project management approach. If we're not careful, it can orient us to a top-down approach, a 'working for' mentality where we don't notice the assets and potential that already exists within our communities. It can also lead us to overfocus on tangible 'results' and forget that it is often the intangible relationships that make the most difference, even if this is hard to measure.

We can address this in (at least) a couple of ways. The first is to work hard to involve those we seek to serve in the design and running of the project itself ('working with' rather than 'working for'). Hannah gave us an example of a church that successfully moved from 'working for' to 'working with': they had started a toy library for parents who were struggling financially. Initially, it was run by volunteers from the more affluent area next to the housing estate they were serving, but now it's run by some of the people who initially came to the library to borrow toys. Hannah explained:

It would have taken some investment in them, but they would also have brought ideas about how to do things better, because they understand the people that might want to use it. They're perfectly capable of running a toy library, but they may not have been given that opportunity before.

Though it can be a challenge to involve people who aren't already 'signed off' as volunteers or as leaders, in Hannah's words 'having agency is actually a really good gift to give someone'. (In fact, sometimes the hardest thing to let go of is our desire to be the one 'helping'!)

That's the first approach. The second approach is to maintain our emphasis on 'being with' and use this as the springboard for other forms of activity. For example, if we run a project providing hot meals for those who are homeless, we can spend a lot of energy involving homeless people in serving and preparing the food (dealing with the food hygiene rules, qualifications and so on). This attempt to make the project more 'working with' than 'working for' is a valid approach, but it's not always the best. The alternative is to realise that the main thing is getting *everyone* around the table eating together: those cooking, those serving and those attending. And really prioritise this. This is 'being with', and that's how conversation and community happens. And out of these conversations, surprising things can emerge.

When we lean into 'being with', projects that meet an immediate need can become excellent building blocks towards wider community transformation. Hannah gave us another example of this from her work: 'Someone had experience working with refugees through community sponsorship,' Hannah shared, 'so they set up a space where people, both hosts and Ukrainian guests, could come and speak English to each other.' The project now had an 'event' to centre it, and the team were consistently connecting with the group, creating a foundation from which to address other issues. As a result, 'they realised people were both in search of jobs and that there was confusion over Universal Credit', so they were then able to take action together on these issues.

In this situation with Ukrainian refugees and Hannah's earlier example of people relocating from Hong Kong, the people involved in the project recognised there was an issue beyond the immediate one they were meeting. They listened to the people who were affected by it, found out what the wider challenges were, and worked on a solution together.

This takes time and can be difficult. Sometimes these wider challenges are tough to crack, and sometimes simply working together as a team, across cultures and when people are in stressful life-situations, can be just as hard! In the end, though, this approach can be transformational, and may even address issues such as the amount of money that people on low incomes are paid (as in the case of the real Living Wage campaign, which Hannah has been working on).

This process of listening and working on solutions together is also known as **community organising**. Hannah shares more:

Something that's really central to community organising is relational power. Citizens UK[4] talks about how the market has financial power; governments and some individuals have positional power; civic society doesn't hold either of those, but when you have a representative group of people, you hold the relational power. If you are able to utilise that relational power, then you can ultimately change things.

Community organising centres on meeting up with people, often one to one, and building relationships. As Hannah says, it means asking: 'Who are you? What do you care about?' rather than just saying: 'Here's what I want to do – let's go and do it.' Citizens UK also have a useful golden rule: 'Never do for others what they can do for themselves.' Once a group coalesces on an issue, it often starts to look and feel like campaigning, but often at a local level. In fact, these things often go hand in hand, as Christine's story illustrated in the previous chapter. Her individual litter-picking project captured the imagination of those around her and developed into a local environmental group, which has then helped influence the local council and MPs to build bike lanes and take more care of the surrounding area.

We want to close this chapter by considering a type of activism that's even closer to home: **hospitality**. This is the main theme of Krish Kandiah's work. He shares:

'Hospitality' is an interesting word. It's used relatively cheaply about an industry that has a transactional relationship: 'You pay £10 and you can have food in my restaurant.' That's the hospitality industry.

But biblical hospitality is modelled on the kindness and compassion of God. It's about making room for someone to be able to be who they are.

Krish has recently been involved in catalysing hospitality for refugees from Ukraine, but most of his work is related to familial hospitality, such as fostering and adoption. He asks, 'What does it mean to welcome children who don't have access to a safe family because of abuse or neglect?' And the answer? 'God tells us that God is a father to the fatherless and places the lonely in families. Those families are our families,' he suggests.

We are often in awe of people who practise this form of activism. There is a profound justice element to it that transcends other forms; at its best it means a reordering of our lives and homes to make space for another person, in a deep expression of love. (However, it's also true that 'hospitality' can be used unhealthily to meet our own needs or to exert power over others.)

When you have a refugee family staying with you, it's a 24/7 commitment, making room for them. When you adopt, it's a lifetime commitment. There's a line in a spoken word written by Katie Dowds that says, 'To be welcomed and to be healed are not so different; that's why we call it hospitality.'[5] If you think back to testimonies that you've heard from people who have overcome trauma and turned their lives around, I expect you'll find that hospitality often plays a role.

Of course, hospitality isn't often easy. It's something that we need to go into with our eyes wide open, out of love rather than a desire to meet our own needs. But it's also something that reflects God's heart for us. Adoption is often referred to as the highest privilege the gospel gives us. Krish reflects: 'If a bank manager forgives your debt, you'll probably never see him again. But adoption is relational; it's about the intimacy God intended for us. It's the restoration of shalom. Practising hospitality in our family made that real.'

Questions for reflection

- Revisit what came up for you in the 'What is God giving you hope for?' exercise in chapter 4. Did this relate to key needs in your community?
- What are the key needs in your community? Note down any ideas you might have about how you could address them. Are there any other organisations or groups near you who are already working in this area?
- If you are already involved in a local project:
  - How is it going? What are the things that are working well, and what is causing stress?
  - Have you spoken to the people you're seeking to serve about how they think it's going? Can you make time to chat to them and hear feedback in the coming week?
  - How can you make space for and maintain the attitude of 'being with' in your project?
- Have you ever come across the idea of hospitality as Krish talks about it? Did his examples and explanation prompt any particular thoughts or questions?
- How could you start to practise hospitality?

Recommended resources

- Paul Blakey's interview 'Street Angels: Action in the wild west of Yorkshire', *Hopeful Activists* podcast, 2 May 2019
- Lara Bundock and Rachel Medina's interviews 'Snowdrop: Wisdom for the road', parts 1 and 2, *Hopeful Activists* podcast, 20 and 27 September 2019
- Citizens UK: citizensuk.org
- Home for Good: homeforgood.org.uk, which supports people to adopt or foster children
- The story of Hope at Home (which supports people to host refugees) on the *Hopeful Activists* podcast; see the episode 'Hope at Home: Starting something new', 6 November 2020. You can also find out more about how to become a host at hopeathome.org.uk.
- If you are looking for funding, the following websites offer affordable subscription services for large-grant databases: www.myfundingcentral.co.uk and www.grantsonline.org.uk. Alternatively, check out your nearest Community Foundation for local grants: www.ukcommunityfoundations.org/our-network. You can also access bespoke fundraising support, as well as organisational development and leadership support, through Futurekraft: futurekraft.org.

8

Who's with me?

You may have heard the saying: 'If you want to travel fast, travel alone; but if you want to travel far, travel in the company of friends.' As we've heard over the past couple of chapters, in order to get anywhere in activism you need people around you. As the writer of Proverbs says:

> As iron sharpens iron,
>   so one person sharpens another.[1]

But if you're thinking of starting something new, who would be the 'right' members of your team? How do you 'do team' well? And what's the best way to join in with a team that already exists? We spoke to Aaron Shah, musician and founder of Worship on the Streets, about how he was supported by the people around him to help equip a national movement of street worshippers, and we asked him about how this could apply to other types of activism.

Before we hear some of Aaron's wisdom, **think about the best experience of team that you've had. What made it so positive?** Then, **think about an experience of team that was all right (not awful). What made it a bit disappointing? What could have improved it?**

***

For me (Rachel), one of the best experiences of team I had was while I was part of the worship group at Encounter Church Selly Oak. We prayed and had fun together; we played good music together; we learned and grew and changed together. Being part of that team was not without its bumpy patches, but it was an experience that had a deep impact on me. The reason the team worked, despite our many cultural and social differences, was that we had a shared vision and we also all genuinely cared for and supported one another. Not only did I learn lots about being a better vocalist and worship leader; I also learned about how much I was loved by God and his people.

I really hope you've experienced something similar! Whether we're starting something new, or joining in with something already running, we need to have people around us whom we trust to give us advice and challenge us, as well as support us with the tricky things.

So how do we find them – and who are they? In this chapter, we'll go through six different groups of people you'll need around you to be effective in activism, hearing some of Aaron's story along the way.

Worship on the Streets started up in the north of England in December 2014 with the aim of making worship accessible to people who didn't go to church: leading street worship locally, and running sessions to equip street worshippers nationally. But the seed of this radical, risky, public idea had taken root a while beforehand. Aaron shared:

We didn't have a grid for this type of ministry. My wife and I had a couple of really close friends who we'd known for years and prayed with regularly together. Years ago, we'd given permission to each other to speak into each other's lives. They knew our stories, our passions, our callings, our strengths and weaknesses. They helped us to think through the impact of starting up Worship on the Streets on our finances, on family life, things like that.

Discernment isn't a one-person process: it's not just you locked away in a small room with a Bible, a journal and God! (Though this can be a helpful part.) Aaron involved his **close friends** in the process of trying to figure out where God was leading him. This is the first group we need around us: people who know us well, who are safe, and who can help us sharpen the vision of what it is we want to do. For Aaron, the wise counsel and prayers of these friends over this period of discernment was hugely significant. 'The outcome was that starting Worship on the Streets felt in line with who God has made me to be, and what he was saying at the time.'

Once we have decided to pursue the vision that we have spent time discerning, where do we turn next? Aaron again:

I spoke to Burn 24/7, a movement who had experience leading worship outside of church contexts. They were people who had more experience than I had who I could ask questions to, people who could help me learn more about the theology specific to my work. Developing your theology around your work builds foundations in your work – the more robust your theology, the more longevity you build.

He sought out those with more experience and wisdom: **people to learn from**. This is the second group of people you'll need around you. For Christine, who wanted to challenge the G7 on their response to the climate crisis, it was clear she needed people like Jack who knew how to start and run a large-scale campaign. She also learned from her peers who had previous experience of speaking to their MPs and organising young people. As for Shane, living in close proximity to those in poverty in Philadelphia, he sought the wisdom and experience of Mother Teresa's community in Kolkata. You may not be needing to seek wisdom about approaching G7 leaders or wanting to learn alongside someone like Mother Teresa, but drawing on the wisdom and hard-earned experience of others is a necessary part of activism.

The third requirement is a **mentor**. At the start of this chapter, I (Rachel) mentioned the worship group I was involved with at church. One of its leaders, Annie Skett, very much inhabited this role for me as I grew in my abilities as a worship leader. She encouraged me and supported me at practices. When things went quite wrong the first time I led the band, she sat with me and asked questions to help me reflect on my leadership and figure out what God might be prompting me to do in other times of worship. She recognised that I had the ability to lead, and helped me to gain the courage to seek and follow God in that.

Aaron shared:

A good mentor doesn't tell you what to do, but asks questions and helps you discern what God is calling you to. I wanted someone who knew me personally and also understood and had experience in the work I was doing. They needed to be someone I trusted, as I would be giving them a lot of access to my life. I didn't rush into this, but over time, it became apparent who the obvious person was for me.

So, at this point, Aaron had close friends helping him through the discernment process, he had people to learn from, and he had a mentor to support him. But he needed something else: **people to join in**. 'Jesus always sent his disciples out in twos – never on their own. It's a good principle. Having people to do stuff with helps to make the work more effective and efficient, enabling it to grow.' This team joined Aaron on the streets as they worshipped and shared the good news of Jesus with those who stopped to listen. They were vital in turning the vision practical.

This brings us to the fifth group of people we need around us: **prayer supporters**. We can again look at the example of Esther, who recognised and said yes to God's call, then immediately asked Mordecai and the rest of the Israelites to pray for her. Aaron described his support network:

For me, I wanted a local group and a wider group. The local group, I would see more regularly; they could see how the ministry was developing and could meet up with me to pray. They all know each other. The wider group are spread all across the nation. They pray for me, with guidance from termly emails and messages on a group chat, and some of them support me financially through the organisation Stewardship.

We also need to think about the longevity of the work we are doing. 'I would add a sixth person to this list: **a person you are training**,' said Aaron. 'My mentor said to me, "Jesus started his ministry by choosing his successors." You need to have an eye out for who might take over from you, if and when you move on.'

So now we have our list! To recap, here are the people you'll ideally have around you to help make your vision a reality for the long term:

- Close friends
- People you learn from
- A mentor
- People to do the stuff with
- Prayer supporters (both local and more broad)
- Someone you are training

Why not take time now to **draw out a support map**. Who are the key people around you? Who is helping with the work itself? Who is most supportive emotionally? Who are you learning from? Who is perhaps a bit difficult? Who would you like to be involved with what you're doing, but isn't?

***

This might all sound pretty straightforward. But, as we all know, working with people can sometimes be the opposite of straightforward! How do we handle it when things don't quite go according to plan?

Another of the *Hopeful Activists* team, Beth Saunders, had an experience like this in her local church. She had a vision to set up a group called Just Church to work on justice issues and mobilise Christians in her area.

When she was setting up the group, she had the help of a life coach and close friend to help her discern the vision and set specific goals. She approached a potential mentor, but they were too busy (as were a couple of others). When she sought people to join in with the vision, she got a really mixed bag:

> Some people were very helpful, but I also got a lot of burnt-out people who had tried similar things before, so I often ended up supporting them. There were also lots of people with ideas but without the time to implement them, as well as some difficult characters! A lot of my time was spent managing people and mentoring them, and in the end I felt burnt out trying to run things and keep everyone happy.

Nevertheless, the group achieved a lot in a couple of years: running Bible studies to help people explore God's call for justice; organising beach clean-ups and litter picks; leading services at their church about food waste, fuel poverty and plastic pollution; getting people involved in national campaigns around these issues; holding film screenings about fast fashion; and partnering with a local food waste / food surplus organisation. After a couple of years, the group came to an end, as Beth no longer had the capacity to run it. This produced mixed feelings in her: 'At the time it felt like a failure, but we achieved a lot in two years, and we finished well.'

Most things are only for a season, and sometimes ending a project can disperse the learning as people go on to get involved in other things, but Beth's experience also prompted some valuable times of growth and reflection. Real life is messy, and often we can't find exactly the team or the support that we want. In this situation, Aaron suggests asking yourself, 'How much can I do with the people I've got?' Beth similarly reflected that addressing some hard questions at the start, such as how much of her time she was ultimately prepared to contribute, would have been valuable. It's really important to ask yourself, 'How much am I prepared to do (or how far am I prepared to go) without having people in place?' It's important to be clear with yourself and with God about this.

Sometimes, the problem isn't a lack of people but the presence of an unhealthy team dynamic! We've all been part of teams that are less than healthy. But how do we help create healthy teams? Think back to the reflection question at the start of the chapter; what can you learn from your answer to that about healthy team culture?

In my (Rachel's) example about my church worship group, it was the fact that (1) we all shared a similar vision and purpose, and (2) we all genuinely cared about one another's growth (and had some fun together!). Ultimately, this was a culture created by my team leaders, Annie and Jack Skett. Setting a culture requires you to model it as a leader. If you want others to be vulnerable, you have to model vulnerability. If you want others to be empowering, you have to empower others. If you want others to be encouraging, you have to be encouraging. This isn't sufficient of course (destructive behaviours can still wreak havoc), but positive team cultures don't happen without it.

Two areas that might require dedicated thought are vulnerability and boundaries. We'll talk a bit more about boundaries in the next chapter, but from a team perspective consider this: how much of your life do you want to share (or is it safe to share) with the rest of the team? Authenticity and vulnerability help to build connection, but emotional safety is also important. Something that has taken me (Rachel) a little while to learn is that you can be good teammates without sharing every aspect of your lives with one another! Nevertheless, being honest about our thoughts and emotions regarding the shared work of the team can be crucial to working well together. A good question to have in your mind is: 'Do my team need to know this piece of information in order for us to work well together today?' In Aaron's case, he maintains different levels of vulnerability and boundaries with the different groups described above:

With my close friends and mentor, I know that each person is invested not just in the ministry but, more importantly, in me and in how I am doing. This means that there is a high level of trust, and I am able to share with a high level of vulnerability – not just about the highs and lows of ministry but also about how I am doing in ministry and outside of ministry. With the team and prayer support group, although within both groups there are people I share life with, on the whole the ministry is the priority. People are coming together because they want to be a part of and support the ministry. We aim to foster a pastoral culture recognising that everyone has things going on in their life outside of the ministry, which we want to celebrate, and also to offer empathy and support when things are challenging, but on the whole our time together is ministry-focused, not pastoral. This, in turn, means there is less vulnerability.

Taking this concept of vulnerability and boundaries a step further, unfortunately some teams do really good things outwardly while being quite destructive for those involved. How do we deal with dysfunctional teams? Aaron shared:

I've been part of teams where I've disagreed with some of what the leader is saying, but I've agreed enough with the core vision and values to contribute. At other times, I've had to say, 'Look, I disagree with the values you are endorsing and living out, so I need to step back.' Be really clear with yourself about what's happening and what you are prepared to put up with. You have the agency to choose.

This comes back to boundaries. To put it bluntly: how much are you willing to put up with?

Aaron had further wisdom to share:

All of this should be about love. That's a good benchmark question: is love really central to the team? Is it founded in love, lived out of love? Is this project still an expression of love, and am I able to engage with it in that way?

Though it is always difficult when teams experience dysfunction, these questions should help us think through what to do when that happens.

Finally, and following on from this, how should we approach getting involved with something that's already running? Sometimes, it's far better to expend our energy in getting involved in an already existing group, rather than starting something new. If you are wondering about this, in addition to what Aaron has said above, we've got a few helpful tips below for starting well:

- Clarify your expectations. What is expected of you? What are you expecting? How long are you committing for? Make sure you can do what you've said you're going to do (don't flake!).
- Communicate well. We can probably all think of times when a miscommunication has led to a mix-up! Make sure you know what is your responsibility, and let people know if for some reason you can't fulfil it.
- Offer more if you can (remember, know your capacity!). If you are able to do not just what's expected but also to help build the vision, to offer ideas or to do more, that's

often really valuable to leaders. So don't hold back if
this is you.
• Be an encourager! Encourage the team and leaders
when good things are happening.

When I (Rachel) was thinking with my husband George
about getting involved with the free English classes our
church was running, we asked if we could go along to a
taster session first, to see what the classes were like and to
get an idea of whether we could give it the necessary time
and energy. This was really helpful! We really enjoyed the
session and found it encouraging and life-giving. We're
now in discussions with the group about how often we can
commit to being part of the team that runs the classes.

One final thought. When my (Rich's) son Nathaniel
comes home from preschool, he's fond of saying, 'Teamwork
makes the dream work.' I think this must be said a lot by
the teachers at tidy-up time at the end of the day! It's a
clichéd expression, but it's true that we can't hope to see
the shalom of God's kingdom take root without joining
in with others around us! We've got to work together to
establish healthy teams and good practices. Take some
time now to reflect on the things Aaron has shared and the
questions below.

Questions for reflection

• Do you feel supported in your current activism?
• Did you agree with needing the six groups Aaron
mentioned? Which of the six groups do you feel you
need at this stage?

- How well are the teams you are part of currently functioning?
- What would a next step in this area look like for you?
  - Who could you ask to support you if you've got a new vision to start something?
  - Or how could you be an encourager to other team members and the team leader if you're already involved in something?
- Do you have healthy boundaries in place as a team leader/member?
- Are you doing too much? Or could you be doing more? Has a sense of obligation – of not being able to say no – become an issue?
- Does your team allow you to use your gifts and passions? Does it align with your visions and values?
- Do you know what is expected of you as a team member?

Recommended resources

- Brené Brown, *Daring Greatly: How the courage to be vulnerable transforms the way we live, love, parent, and lead* (New York, NY: Penguin, 2013)
- Henry Cloud and John Townsend, *Boundaries: When to say yes, how to say no, to take control of your life* (Grand Rapids, MI: Zondervan, 2002)
- Danny Silk, *Keep Your Love On: Connection, communication and boundaries* (Loving on Purpose, 2015)
- Pete Scazzero, 'Chapter 8: Power and Wise Boundaries' episode, *The Emotionally Healthy Leader* podcast, 30 July 2019

- Patrick Lencioni, '18. How Dysfunctional Is Your Team?' episode, *At The Table with Patrick Lencioni* podcast, 12 December 2019
- Patrick Lencioni, '1. What Is Your Genius?' episode, *The Working Genius* Podcast with Patrick Lencioni, 23 February 2021

9

Love and (how to avoid) burnout

There's a moment towards the end of the book *The Boy, the Mole, the Fox and the Horse* where the titular boy reflects on the purpose of life: "'I've realised why we are here," whispered the boy. "For cake?" asked the mole. "To love," said the boy.'[1]

This is the premise on which the first eight chapters of this book have been written (the foundational importance of love – and perhaps also of cake). It's where we started back in chapter 1, with the primacy of love, with all of the Old Testament law being summed up as 'Love the Lord your God with all your passion and prayer and muscle and intelligence – and love your neighbor as well as you do yourself.'[2] It's why we started with Paul's shocking statement in 1 Corinthians that 'if I have a faith that can move mountains, but do not have love, I am nothing. If I give all I possess to the poor . . . but do not have love, I gain nothing.'[3]

However, 'to love' is emphatically not our whole purpose. In Mackesy's book, the horse responds to the boy: '*And be loved.*'[4]

Ultimately, our ability to love others is interwoven with our ability to receive love. And, in particular, to abide in

God and his love. Our ability to receive love is also key to avoiding burnout, which is an ever more common experience for activists these days.

In fact, I (Rich) am writing this a couple of months after coming close to burnout myself. I was working on the project I've referred to elsewhere in this book, pressing for global corporations to show greater respect for the human rights of some of the most marginalised people in the world – the informal workers who collect plastic and other types of waste. I was working longer hours than usual, but the exhaustion mostly came from the emotional strain of trying to stand in the gap between some of the world's most marginalised and some of the world's most powerful, trying to build bridges, taking a fair bit of heat, getting pulled in all directions, and having to make finely balanced decisions under a cloud of uncertainty.

The experience of burnout is different for different people, but in our experience it often means that we push ourselves so hard that we start to experience physical and physiological symptoms (such as severe exhaustion). There are emotional symptoms too, but these are sometimes easier to suppress, so it is the physical symptoms that are often what you notice initially. Thankfully, I recognised the warning signs and was able to take evasive action.

Clearly, sacrifice is part of how we are supposed to live as followers of Jesus. Part of our role as Christians is to 'participate in the sufferings of Christ'[5] as we face brokenness and injustice, and work alongside him to bring healing and restoration. Paul talks about us being 'living sacrifices',[6] and Jesus lived a life of tremendous sacrifice, even before the crucifixion. So is burnout just part of the Christian experience? Or is there a way to hold sacrifice together with the fact that Jesus came so that we could 'have life, and have it to the full'?[7]

We met Jan de Villiers in chapter 3 – the founder of youth charity e:merge and the social enterprise Futurekraft, which has helped incubate and develop more than 150 justice projects, particularly around Bradford. He is no stranger to burnout, and we asked him about his experience. This is what he shared:

> As a young man, I was quite a zealot to 'go and proclaim the gospel in all the world'. No sacrifice was too much. I'm quite a passionate person; I do throw myself into what I choose to do. So for me, there was a real physical element to sacrifice: I gave up all that I had, jacked in my job, went into missions. I trusted God like in the scripture where Jesus sends out his disciples without a purse, just with the clothes on their back. That was the kind of sacrifice that meant something to me – that is what, to me, all Christians should have done.
>
> But we grow up in ourselves, physically, emotionally, spiritually. Right now, my view of sacrifice is this: I think all of us have been called, and all of us have purpose. We are learning about our purpose along this journey in life. God does the inner work in us. We each fill a space that is unique to us. Sacrifice in that context is knowing your calling, your purpose, and being true to that.

Jan highlights the importance of understanding our specific calling – the difference between the view that we must do the maximum to 'bring God's kingdom' and the view that we should be faithful to the *specific role* that God has given us. This makes a big difference. It seems obvious, but sometimes we forget that we can never meet all the need we see around us. Instead, our role is to be faithful to the calling God has given us: to become the person he has made us to be (as we talked about in chapter 3).

I (Rachel) recognise a lot of what Jan shared about his younger self in my own story. I used to work for a global Christian missionary organisation, inspired by the idea of building God's kingdom and working for him. I always found it hard, even though I loved the people I worked with and had believed in what we were doing. But towards the end of my time there, the responsibilities of my role got exceptionally tough. I couldn't manage the day-to-day tasks, let alone the long-term ones, and it was having a hugely negative effect on my health. I rationalised it to myself, telling myself that God had called me to the organisation and that the pain and difficulty I was feeling were part of the necessary sacrifice to follow his call. I needed to 'take up my cross';[8] I just needed to push through this next bit of difficulty. Jesus hadn't promised me an easy life, right?

It took months of me getting steadily more fragile before some good friends said over a pub lunch, 'Rach, we don't think it's meant to be this painful and hard to just go to work. We don't think this is what God has for you.' Somehow, though others (including my parents) had been concerned, it was their words that hit home. I took a step back and spent a while asking God if he was really wanting me to make this type of sacrifice to build his kingdom. Turns out, he wasn't – and I handed in my notice shortly after that, stepping into the unknown to find out what he did want me to do. My workplace generously gave me a sabbatical before leaving, so I had three months off to rest, recover and spend time figuring out what my role was (and is) in God's story.

Ultimately, our calling is to uncover and embrace the unique reflection of God that he has placed in each one of us. As Thobes said, it's 'finding the freedom to be fully who God called you to be'. It goes without saying that this doesn't mean choosing the easiest, most comfortable life. Jan shared:

> I'm called to work in inner-city deprived areas, and Futurekraft is all about developing communities of hope. That's our purpose. I can look over the fence sometimes and go, 'These middle-class people have it so nice – I want to be like that!' But sacrifice is holding on to your purpose, holding on to that vision that you are called to. And that's hard.

This realisation entails a recognition that, in Jan's words, 'it's not all about the stuff that we do; it's about *being*: being in this world, being transformed on a daily basis (as Shane said in chapter 3). That's the calling. That's how we become light to the world.' When we are on this journey of becoming, we are able to challenge injustice *both* through what we do *and* through who we are, and we are also more resilient to burnout. We need to be open to this growth and change in order to find the freedom of being the person God made us to be.

Here are two reflection questions to help you ground this in your own experiences:

- **What is God teaching you about yourself at the moment?**
- **How would you describe 'the person God has called you to be'?**

***

Related to this tension between 'doing' and 'becoming' is another key distinction that was a real epiphany for me (Rich), and completely reoriented how I see our role in the world. It's the difference between *pouring ourselves out* in the service of justice and *seeking to overflow* with the love and grace of God in the specific place and role that he gives us.

Remember in chapter 2, we heard Lisa's insight that in our experience, 'rivers are made up of small streams that converge. But the four rivers in Eden spring from the garden, then separate and flow outward! This is the essence of abundance: flowing outwards.'[9] And throughout his ministry, we see abundant life flowing out of Jesus in the same way. We are invited into this way of being and doing.

When we lean away from 'pouring out' and lean towards 'overflow', the timbre of our activity is very different. I'm an economist by training, and basic economics (and indeed our culture) tells us that if we can just work harder – put in more effort and more resources – then we will see more change. This isn't about overflow, though; instead it's the language of industrial production. It's a mathematical equation, where more effort and input equals more output. This mindset dominates our world so much that it has even affected how we see activism (even for those working against the injustices of capitalism! Oh, the irony). If we buy into it, then clearly, we have to work ourselves to the bone to achieve the maximum possible.

By contrast, when we think about overflow, it's not long before we start thinking about the scriptural picture of fruitfulness that we see in Psalm 1: about a tree planted by a clear stream, 'which yields its fruit in season'.[10]

Fruitfulness is the natural result of the growth of a tree that is planted in the right place. The tree doesn't produce fruit on its own, but through drawing on the life and energy around it in a natural, organic process. Jesus uses the same analogy for our relationship with him: 'If you remain in me and I in you, you will bear much fruit; apart from me you can do nothing.'[11] In Jesus' model, it is our rootedness in him (rather than the number of hours we put in) that is the most important determinant of fruitfulness.

Bringing effective change has more to do with fruitfulness than it does with the language of industrial production. The industrial production mindset has helped drive some of the biggest injustices we face: climate change, biodiversity loss and inequality, to name but three. So it seems unlikely that we can solve these problems without living in a different way – modelling a different way of being, rather than simply redirecting the world's model of doing.

Here's a **practical exercise** to help you ground this. Take a piece of paper and draw a line down the middle. On the left, write down all the things that are life-giving in a typical month for you (with each in its own little bubble) – the things that help you connect to God and receive his love, the things that bring you joy, laughter and energy. Then on the right, put down all the things that are life-draining right now, including both things you regard as 'activism' and everything else from the rest of your life. Is there a balance, or an imbalance? How do you feel about that?

***

Let's bring all of this back to burnout and put it into a framework for thinking about how to avoid it. We're going to use a 'transformation triangle', which is an idea we've borrowed from Krish Kandiah. Krish suggests that transformation in our lives often results from three things:

- Changes in the narratives we tell ourselves about who we are and why we're here – our world view
- Our praxis; in other words, how we put into practice what we believe
- The community that we do that with

Let's unpack this triangle a bit . . .

1 World view

So far in this chapter, we've been talking a lot about our world view. Do you subscribe more to the industrial production paradigm than to the fruitfulness paradigm when you think about how to work for justice? To put it another way, to what extent do you think *who you become* is more important than *what you do*?

These beliefs have tangible impacts on how we live. For instance, I (Rich) have learned that I shouldn't apologise for the fun and beauty in my life, because I need those life-giving things in order to bring life to and through my activism.

Our beliefs also affect how we handle struggle and difficulty. It's unusual to be an activist, or indeed a human being, without experiencing failure to some degree! And if we think that what we *do* is by far the most important thing, then failure has few redeeming qualities: we have failed to 'do' the thing that we set out to do. Failure can even become a challenge to our core identity as a person if our sense of self has become bound up with what we do. However, if we are focused on *becoming*, then our actions are one expression of our identity, but our identity itself is not bound up with them. Instead, in this mindset, failure can be part of our journey of becoming – the uncomfortable furnace in which godly character is formed.

2 Praxis

Often, our lives don't match up with our beliefs! Paul talks about this in Romans: 'what I want to do I do not do, but what I hate I do.'[12] This is where the second side of our transformation triangle comes in: our praxis. When it comes to outworking our world view, it's helpful to have a set of rhythms and practices to follow – like a trellis or set of garden canes that guide and support us as we grow into the person God has made us to be. These practices will look different for each of us, because we're all different! However, there may be a few things we have in common.

Perhaps the most important practice of all is setting **good boundaries**. The research professor, social worker and author Brené Brown said that one of the most shocking findings from her research was that 'the most compassionate people . . . were also the most boundaried'.[13] Setting good boundaries – saying no to things, prioritising space to connect to God, yourself, those close to you; making time for life-giving activities; deciding what is 'too much'; all these things are deeply connected with maintaining our ability to be compassionate.

Boundaries are the natural outworking of both a fruitfulness mindset and a recognition that, as Jan says, 'ultimately it is more about becoming our true selves than about what we do'. Boundaries mean making time for things that give us life. Boundaries mean saying no to things that aren't consistent with our growth or with becoming the person God is asking us to be.

Practical exercise. With boundaries in mind, now would be a good time to draw together three of the previous practical exercises from this book:

- The life-giving/life-draining exercise from a couple of pages ago
- The two mind maps from chapter 4, which addressed the questions 'What am I currently involved with?'

and 'What am I passionate about? What is God
highlighting to me?'

Look at the things described on these charts. Are there
any areas where you think different boundaries need to be
imposed? Are there any that you might even need to phase
out completely? (If you think there are, but find it hard to
say no to people, then it's worth discussing it with a friend
and working out exactly how you are going to go about
pulling back. Sharing in this way will help to give you both
courage and accountability.)

***

Good boundaries often underpin many of our other
rhythms and practices: they are the stakes that hold up the
trellis. So what other rhythms might we adopt?

Recently, we reviewed all the interviews we've carried
out with activists and theologians over the last few years –
more than 100 of them (mostly conducted by our amazing
friend and colleague Abi Thomas). We realised that, above
everything else that they had said, the most common piece
of advice was to adopt regular practices of connecting to
God; this means dedicated time – daily, weekly, monthly,
yearly practices.

Shane Claiborne explained it with an example from his
activism against gun violence:

We've been melting guns and turning them into
garden tools. I love this work – you take this hard,
cold metal from the barrel of a gun or a knife, and

put it into the fire. It begins to take on the character of the fire; it begins to glow so that you can't even tell the metal from the fire. It begins to blend into it – that's what softens the metal and allows it to be moulded and changed. If you take it out too long, it begins to harden again and you can crack it. So you've got to keep bringing it back to the fire. In this work it's easy to get cold and hardened and tired. And that's why we've got to keep returning to the fire of God's love. We've got to keep near to Jesus.

Edwin Arrison, a close friend of the veteran anti-apartheid activist Archbishop Desmond Tutu, shared about the archbishop's daily rhythms:

The Arch was very close to God every single day. What he did and what he said publicly was born and nurtured in many, many hours of silence, in the daily Eucharist . . . that's where it all started. I would really want to encourage Christian activists to make time for silence.[14]

Shane also shared about the change he and his community went through:

Maybe ten years into the Simple Way community and the little movement we have going over here in the US, we began to realise that we were better activists than we were in our own prayer life and spirituality. That's where the Common Prayer project rose out of, the desire to have some rhythms for prayer each day that connected our prayer life with what's going on in the world. We remember dates that are both some of the most tragic dates in history, and we also remember the great victories – when Mandela was released from prison, when Rosa Parks went to jail, all those things. There's also really great spiritual exercises in there that are tried and true. We've got prayers that are over a thousand years old. We pray for the fruit of the Spirit, and I pray the Lord's Prayer a lot. I think there's a lot to unpack in it. So I go through it slowly and deliberately.

Our practices can change and evolve. For me (Rachel), these practices have changed quite a bit over the last year, as I've adjusted from being single to being married. I've also gone from being involved in a Charismatic church community to one that faithfully goes through the Anglican liturgy! My husband, George, and I have found it helpful to read through the morning prayer service from the Book of Common Prayer at the start of each day, and often do the evening prayer service before we go to bed. I love music, so I enjoy taking time to listen (and sometimes sing along at home) to hymns and sung worship, particularly on Tube journeys across London. The thing that helps me most concentrate on God and talk to him, though, is getting out and walking around my local park for my morning 'commute' before my day working from home; I find I'm able to breathe, realise the things that are on my mind, and pray specifically for them.

Jo Musker-Sherwood, who, following her own experience of burnout, now researches resilience strategies for climate activists, highlights four daily practices that she has adopted: grace, grounding, gratitude and growth. She takes ten minutes in stillness to meditate or pray (grace); does an activity to get out of her head and focus on the world around her, such as dancing or smelling something lovely (grounding); writes down ten things at the end of every day that she is thankful for (gratitude); and takes some time to 'journal' – to write down her thoughts and feelings, and process where she is going (growth).[15]

Practical exercise. Which rhythms and practices do you find most helpful in your activism and your walk with God? Are there any that you would like to experiment with adopting?

3 Community

In chapter 8 we talked a lot about the importance of community for starting new projects and sustaining us. It's so important that it's worth underlining here as the third side of the transformation triangle. As Rachel shared earlier in this chapter, describing the experience she had at her former workplace, sometimes those closest to us see what is going on with us clearer than we can ourselves. Community can also keep us accountable. If you have new practices that you want to adopt from the previous exercise, why not mention them to a close friend so they can ask you how you are getting on in a week or two?

Living and working in community also gives us extra resources and wisdom to draw on when things get hard. Shane illustrates it this way:

The way that you put out a fire, a campfire, is you scatter the coals. And the way that you keep a fire alive is by stoking those coals. That's why community and movement are so essential. If you're just a little candle, you can be blown out by the wind, but a fire is actually fuelled by the wind. When the winds come, it only makes the fire stronger.

***

The transformation triangle can be used to help implement many of the things that we've talked about throughout this book. It helps us to be intentional about changes in our world view, making sure they are supported by a trellis of rhythms and practices, and by a community, that will lead to wider change in our life.

We are here to love and be loved: to know, deeply, the love of God and to share that with others. It is in that overflow that we can participate in the hope and transformation that Jesus brings to the world. We can see his shalom take root in the world around us! We can be hopeful activists not just now, but for the rest of our lives.

Questions for reflection

- Do you think you strike a good balance between activities that are life-giving (the things that help you connect to God and receive his love, the things that bring you joy, laughter and energy) and those that are life-draining (including both things you regard as 'activism' and everything else from the rest of your life)?

- What do you think of the difference between operating out of a fruitfulness mindset and operating out of an 'industrial production' mindset when it comes to our activism?
- What is God teaching you about yourself at the moment?
- How would you describe 'the person God has called you to be'?
- Bring together your reflections on life-giving versus life-draining activities with the two mind maps discussed in chapter 4 (which addressed the questions 'What am I currently involved with?' and 'What am I passionate about? What is God highlighting to me?'). Look at the things described on these charts. Are there any areas where you think different boundaries need to be imposed? Are there any that you might even need to phase out completely?
- Which rhythms and practices do you find most helpful in your activism and your walk with God? Are there any that you would like to experiment with adopting? (If you have new practices that you want to adopt, why not mention them to a close friend so they can ask you how you are getting on in a week or two?)

Recommended resources

- Tony Horsfall's interview 'Going Deeper: Wisdom for the road', *Hopeful Activists* podcast, 6 September 2019

- Jo Musker-Sherwood's interview 'How to Stay Well When the World Is Burning', *Hopeful Activists* podcast, 9 July 2021
- 'Lessons from 100 Christian Activists' episode, *Hopeful Activists* podcast, 29 July 2022
- Dina Glouberman, *The Joy of Burnout: How the end of the world can be a new beginning* (Shanklin: Skyros Books, 2002)

10

Conclusion: When the rubber hits the road

Where do we go from here? I (Rachel) don't know how you're feeling as you get to the end of the book. Hopefully you are inspired and encouraged to go and do what God is calling you to do! Maybe, though, you're feeling as if there's been a lot of information to take in, and you're wondering how some of it translates into practical action. I have certainly felt like that before!

Knowing this, we wanted to end the book with two stories from ordinary, hopeful activists who grappled with the same kind of material as you have read here, then put it into practice and saw God at work.

Meet Alison, who helped to start a community fridge – a place where people could bring unwanted food for storage, and anyone else could come to take it. She recalls how it first began:

> I went to a Tearfund Action community event, quite reluctantly – I felt I was too old and didn't have enough influence. I was a bit lacking in faith! I said to God that I wasn't committing to anything beyond the weekend, but he had different plans. I went away from that weekend inspired by the things

that people had already done and were determined to do.

Having thought before the weekend that she didn't think much could ever be changed, Alison went home wanting to start something herself:

> I set up a small group in my church using some of the biblical study materials that had been recommended. This resulted in us doing a number of one-off events (including inviting our local MP to a panel debate at our church), but I was asking God, 'Isn't there something more long-term that is going to come out of this?' At that time I read about community fridges, and it felt like things clicked: it was environmental because it was preventing food waste and all the emissions associated with that; but it was also addressing poverty, because it was feeding people who were going to need it. Doing the Praxis course [similar to the material in this book] gave me the confidence I needed to get started.

Alison wrote to her local town centre manager, not expecting a positive response. However, the manager agreed to meet, and following discussions over a few months, she agreed to let Alison have an empty shop to put her fridge in. Some time later, though, after waiting on tenterhooks and getting started on the organising, Alison received the unwelcome news that the whole shopping centre had been sold for redevelopment.

I was asking God, 'What are you doing? Why did you lead me up this garden path?' I felt like a fool: I had told people that I thought God was in the setting-up of the fridge and tried to encourage them to get involved. I had a day of prayer to see if I could figure out what God was doing, and I didn't hear much except having a sense that God was battling beside me, and I had to keep battling through.

A couple of months later, Alison was chatting to some good friends who had just moved to become part of a church plant on a local estate. They shared how they sometimes had children turning up at their youth group who hadn't had enough to eat, so were very enthusiastic about the community fridge idea!

They picked up the ball and ran with it. They are exactly the sort of people that you really want on your team. Neil is a retired maths teacher and is incredibly organised; Liz is one of those people that can persuade anyone to do anything. She persuaded the local franchise of a national sandwich shop to donate a huge commercial fridge, Neil got a load of people organised, and in January 2020 we started out of a portable cabin in the church car park, with end-of-day contributions from the sandwich shop and a popular bakery chain.

Things were going well and they were getting about a dozen regular people coming along each time – and then March

Conclusion

2020 arrived, when the UK went into lockdown because of the Covid-19 pandemic. The community fridge shut its doors for a few weeks, and Alison began volunteering to do admin at a local food bank. The food bank started getting calls from restaurants and cafés, asking if they would like donations of fresh food that would otherwise go to waste because of the Covid restrictions, but the food bank wasn't equipped to store or give out fresh food. Alison describes what happened next:

I spoke to Neil, and he got it organised. Liz phoned up all the local shops and restaurants asking if they had any leftover food, and we collected it all into the portable cabin. We also joined the FareShare scheme, collecting end-of-day donations from local supermarkets. We laid it all out on trestle tables in the church car park, and sent the news around the estate, not knowing if anyone would come – but people just flocked to it. We would open at 9:15, but people started queuing up before eight o'clock beside the church. We had noise complaints from the neighbours about people chatting in the queue! But another lady across the road came and asked if she could help, and then about ten other local people, not involved in the church, also came along and wanted to help. It exploded beyond all my imagining. We have forty to sixty people coming every Wednesday and Saturday, and about twenty-five regulars who are forming their own community. It's something that I could never have pictured at the start.

Since then, they have done 350 food distributions – involving around fifteen collections of donations per week – and have distributed more than a tonne of food per month. Alison shares:

The highlight is the feeling that the community is coming together. The lady across the road who first wanted to get involved is now starting a community garden in the church grounds too. Three other churches have come along to see what we're doing and have started their own projects. The Michelin-starred restaurant local to us gave us eighty food hampers at Christmas to distribute to those who would need it, and the local chippy provided free fish and chips to the schoolkids who would miss out on free school meals over half term.

The community fridge has also become an informal information point for people to access other resources, such as tools for living well on a tight budget, finding work and getting help with debt, and there are ongoing conversations about how to address the lack of quality housing locally. Once Covid-19 rules permitted, we were able to open the church after Fridge time for coffee and chat. Genuine friendships and support have come from this.

There have been some amazing highlights, but it's not been without its challenges either:

Most people are really lovely, but there can be a certain amount of arguing about whether someone got more than someone else, or whether someone always gets to the front of the queue and gets the best bits. The helpers and other people in the queue have sometimes experienced abusive language. Some of the Fridge members have problems with addiction or mental health issues. We faced real challenges during Covid-19 when we had to go indoors because of bad weather and had to really police things [making sure people kept to social distancing and other rules]. But I have learned so much from God and from others. My advice is to keep going: keep listening to God and keep on going. What has happened is so much better than what I thought of originally.

Alison's story of starting the community fridge highlights several themes we can learn from: persevering when things get tough, taking time out for prayer, finding the right people to be on the team, being bold enough to push for ideas that might feel a little foolish at first, and trusting God even when the path looks unclear.

What strikes *you* about Alison's story?

***

Alison's experience is an example of setting up a new local project, but there are many other ways to follow our calling to counter injustice and pursue shalom. For Jen, whom we spoke to on the *Hopeful Activists* podcast, adoption is a big part of this call, alongside really living out the value of 'proximity' that both Krish and Shane talked about earlier in the book.[1] In the case of our podcast producer

Abi, activism has taken many forms: hosting refugees, organising a local campaign to address a significant source of local air pollution (parents waiting outside the local school with their car engines running), helping out at various local projects and, of course, producing the podcast!

Lau Ciocan, another graduate of our Praxis Labs course, gives us another example: 'According to UK government data, men are around three times more likely to die by suicide than women. The reasons behind this are complex, but a restrictive view of masculinity certainly contributes to the men's mental health epidemic.' For some time, Lau searched for answers to the question 'What are the healthy traits of masculinity?', and felt as though he started to find some answers during the first Covid-19 lockdown. As a result, in May 2020, he set up Mentoring Advocacy Network (MAN), a platform raising awareness of men's mental health and healthy masculinities through public speaking, webinars and later the *Mentality* podcast.

Key to the founding of MAN was the realisation that men can't carry on with unexamined traumas and distorted views of manhood that are self-destructive. As Lau says:

A restrictive view of masculinity is a mental straitjacket that makes it harder for men to reach out and ask for help when they face mental health challenges. As a society, we are all too aware of the adverse effects of a restrictive and toxic view of masculinity for men and how it negatively impacts others. Setting up MAN, I wanted to shape the narrative around healthy masculinities and leave a more wholesome legacy for future generations of men and boys.

One of the things that helped him in his journey as MAN grew organically over time was the realisation that 'there's no formula for activism, but there is a Father for it': God is with us, each step on the journey. And all the hard work hasn't gone unnoticed. In June 2023, Lau was nominated for the Future Leader Award, and MAN for the Best Men's Health Initiative, by the InsideOut Awards, an organisation championing those active in the mental health ecosystem. And in August 2023, Lau delivered a TEDx talk in London on the nuances of masculinity.

There is no formula, and the number of different forms of activism is really as large as the number of activists out there!

Now, though, we'd like you to meet (a different!) Rachel, who co-founded the Young Christian Climate Network (YCCN):

My story is that when I was younger, I didn't care about the environment. And then, when I went to university, I had some friends at church who changed my mind on that; they said that they cared for the environment because they were Christian, and it had an impact on how they lived. It really convicted me! And a little bit after that I read the line from Hans Küng, that 'the kingdom is God's creation healed'. It's a really holistic picture of redemption. Part of my shift into understanding that caring for the environment was part of faith was understanding that my faith wasn't just an individual thing (about my life beyond death) but was much, much wider.

After leaving university, Rachel spent a year working in Parliament in London, getting involved in church and getting involved in climate activism. Feeling a little like an outsider in non-Christian friendship groups for being a Christian, and in Christian groups for being interested in climate activism, she wanted to find people who shared some of the passion that she had for Jesus and creation. Shortly after that, she moved to Sheffield to pursue working in creation care with Hope for the Future.

> In January, I was speaking with someone from USPG [United Society Partners in the Gospel], and they were asking if I could point them to younger Christians who were active on climate change. I told them that apart from the couple of people they had already named, I couldn't think of anyone obvious. The conversation stayed with me because I felt like there really should be a better answer to give than that.

Shortly after that, the pandemic hit. Rachel describes her response:

> I'm an extrovert, and I really missed being able to see people and felt a huge loss at my calendar emptying out. But I felt I also had the time to think intentionally about what I might want to do with the extra time.

She decided to use some of that time to start a group of young Christians who cared about the climate.

> I gathered together some different people I knew and asked whether they would be up for meeting up once a week to have some conversations about environment issues, and seeing where it might go. Some people didn't understand it, or didn't think it was a good idea; others were really keen and thought we really needed it! I'm going to remember that for the future, because I don't think there is an idea that 100% of people are going to be on board with. But that's where YCCN started – with those weekly conversations throughout the pandemic.

The group then went on to organise a 1,200-mile pilgrimage from Cornwall (where the G7 leaders were meeting) to Glasgow, in time for COP26, asking leaders to 'Rise to the Moment' and commit to better financial support for countries already affected by climate change. It received a lot of support from churches and other organisations, as well as media coverage, and people were invigorated and encouraged to ask their leaders for a greater commitment to the climate. Rachel shares:

> One of the joys is that you can do so much more together than you can by yourself, and it's a lot of fun seeing different people bringing their skills and ideas together. It's exciting to not really know where things are going to go! It's a real joy to me too to see people

feel the same thing that you feel, when something suddenly has life beyond the life that you're giving it. Seeing people who are younger than I am do amazing stuff, and knowing that the Network was the reason that the opportunities existed, was amazing.

A project of this scale wasn't without its challenges:

I found it hard not to take things personally! When you don't know the direction something is going in, and when things get bigger, beyond your control, but it still reflects on you, that's really hard. I was surprised by just how vulnerable I felt for quite a long time, through the set-up and launch of YCCN and the Relay [as the pilgrimage was known]. It can also be a challenge when others don't grasp the vision with quite the same passion that you have, or don't want to commit to something in the same way that you have. But respecting people and where they are at is important – even when things get messy, and stuff hasn't been done that you were told would be done. But you've just got to carry on going. Anything worth doing is worth doing badly. You shouldn't let yourself be paralysed in wanting to avoid the risk of doing something wrong.

Rachel has since stepped back from leading YCCN and has seen it grow apart from her. 'It's strange seeing it through other people's eyes! It just grows – both in the number of people involved, and in the meaning that it has for those people. It's cool to see.'

Rachel's story has some similarities to Alison's, but it also covers ground that is completely different. Her point about vulnerability is an important one, and something that I (Rich) have felt too, with the campaigns that I've been involved with starting. What sticks out to you?

***

You've heard Rachel's and Alison's stories, as well as the stories of the other activists whose wisdom we've heard throughout this book. Now it's your turn. What are the inklings of ideas that you feel tugging at you? What areas of injustice are calling for your attention and energy? How can you get involved with God's grand story to bring shalom to all creation?

We hope that this book has given you fuel for the fire, tools for your toolkit. We pray that it will help you to learn to love, to seek God's kingdom and to live the questions – that it will help you be a hopeful activist.

Acknowledgements

There are a significant number of people without whom this book would not have been written.

Billie: thanks for seeing the potential in the idea for the Praxis Labs course, and helping make it a reality. We realise now that you have played the same essential role for many other ideas and many other activists over the years!

Abi: the *Hopeful Activists* podcast has come a long way since a random conversation at a Bradford toddler group! Your energy, insight and radio wizardry are foundational to what we do; thank you.

Beth: thanks for joining when we had no money (!) and then staying for the long haul. You have made the Labs courses so much better (and consequently, this book too).

Thank you also to the rest of the wonderful team at the Praxis Centre for Hope and Activism: Jen, Rebecca, Marcos, Jan, Sue and Eilidh. We couldn't have done this without your continual support, encouragement and investment. Thank you for being all-round good eggs.

Thank you to our contributors and all those who helped arrange interviews: Aaron Shah, Alison Dennis, Anna Boocock, Athena Stevens, Chris Lane, Christine Meyer, Hannah Ling, Jack Wakefield, Jan de Villiers, Katie Kirkpatrick, Katie Zimmerman, Krish Kandiah, Lau Ciocan, Lisa Sharon Harper, Naureen Akhtar, Nick Smith, Rachel Mander, Rhoda Hardie, Ruth Valerio, Sam Wells, Shane Claiborne and Thobes Ncube. Thanks also to all our guests on the podcast over the years; there are too many to mention here, but your words have shaped these pages. Our thanks, too, to all those who have been on the Praxis Labs courses. Your engagement and feedback have also helped to shape this material.

We also want to thank Elizabeth Neep (formerly of SPCK) for believing in the potential of a manuscript written by two debut authors, as well as Katherine Venn and Philip Law at SPCK.

I (Rich) would like to thank my wife and best friend Sophie. A lot of what is in this book we have learned together over nearly twenty years of trying to 'really live and really love' in this broken world. It is a privilege and a pleasure to journey beside you. (And thanks too for summarising all those theology books for me!) Thanks also to Aidan and Nathaniel, who have done a lot to help me learn to love.

I (Rachel) would like to thank my husband, George, who coped remarkably well with being greeted by a slightly stir-crazy, middle-of-the-writing-process version of his new wife most evenings in autumn 2022. Thanks for making me tea, for always loving and encouraging me, and for helping me to work out those tricky paragraphs in the theology chapter. Thanks too to my parents for always being supportive of my writing and for cheering me on to do the things I've been made to do.

Above all, we want to thank God for leading and guiding us throughout this process. To him be the glory. We can't wait to see how his story will unfold.

Notes

Foreword

1 See Isaiah chapter 58; the quotation is from verse 10.
2 See Revelation chapters 21 and 22.

Chapter 1

1 The concept behind 'living the questions' was first outlined in a letter from the poet Rainer Maria Rilke, written in 1903.
2 The Northumbria Community is a dispersed network of Christians from different streams and backgrounds exploring new monasticism together and living by one rule: their calling to availability and vulnerability to God and others. Find out more at www. northumbriacommunity.org.
3 Kenneth E. Bailey, *Jesus through Middle Eastern Eyes: Cultural studies in the Gospels* (Downers Grove, IL: InterVarsity Press, 2008), pp. 280–1.
4 Luke 10:25–37 MSG.
5 1 Corinthians 13:2–4.
6 Corrie Ten Boom, with John and Elizabeth Sherrill, *The Hiding Place* (London: Hodder & Stoughton, 2004), p. 46.
7 Krish Kandiah, with Miriam Kandiah, *Home for Good: Making a difference for vulnerable children* (London: Hodder & Stoughton, 2013).
8 1 Corinthians 13:13.

Chapter 2

1 Genesis 1:1.

2 Revelation 21:4–5.

3 Matthew 1:23.

4 For more on this, see the BibleProject video 'Shalom / Peace', YouTube, 30 November 2017: https://youtu.be/ oLYORLZOaZE (accessed 5 December 2022).

5 See Isaiah 9:6–7. Lisa Sharon Harper, whom we interviewed for this book, has written a great book all about shalom, called *The Very Good Gospel: How everything wrong can be made right* (New York, NY: WaterBrook, 2016). Check it out!

6 You can read the biblical account of this in Genesis chapters 1 and 2. Whether we interpret the creation narrative of the early chapters of Genesis as allegory or as a more literal account, it still contains the same truths about God's purpose for creation. We can also see the difference between this purpose and the reality we experience today.

7 And yet there is a role for humanity here. There is work to do. In Genesis 1:26–8, God makes men and women in God's image and gives them dominion (in Hebrew, *radah*) as his image-bearers. Though they are in the garden of Eden, they are 'to work it and take care of it' (Genesis 2:15). (What's more, the existence of a garden presupposes the existence of areas of 'non-garden' beyond it . . .)

8 Genesis 3:1 (our italics).

9 Harper, *The Very Good Gospel*, p. 45.

10 The rest of creation and other humans are designed to be in shalom relationship with God, but these relationships have also been affected by sin (which Lisa Sharon Harper defines as 'anything that breaks the relationships that

God declared *tov me'od* in the beginning' (*The Very Good Gospel*, p. 48)).

11 It's worth saying that the 'promised land', while bringing hope, is also a challenging part of the story, since the taking of this land meant the displacement of the people already living there – something that we are still seeing the implications of today.

12 The term 'Pentateuch' simply means 'five books': the first five books of the Hebrew Bible, which are traditionally known in Judaism as the Torah.

13 See Colossians 1:15.

14 Genesis 3:15.

15 This is referenced in John 1:3–4.

16 Acts 2:24.

17 Hebrews 2:14.

18 Harper, *The Very Good Gospel*, p. 41.

19 John 4:13–14.

20 Luke 4:16–21.

21 Matthew 6:9–10.

22 Revelation 21:1–4.

23 N. T. Wright, *Surprised by Hope: Rethinking heaven, the resurrection, and the mission of the Church* (London: SPCK, 2008), p. 293.

24 C. S. Lewis, *The Last Battle* (London: Diamond, 1999), p. 366. *The Last Battle* by C. S. Lewis © copyright 1956 CS Lewis Pte Ltd. Extract used with permission.

25 Martin Luther King Jr, 'A Realistic Look at the Question of Progress in the Area of Race Relations', address delivered at St Louis freedom rally, 10 April 1957, The Martin Luther King, Jr. Research and Education

Institute, Stanford University: kinginstitute.stanford.
edu/king-papers/realistic-look-question-progress-area-
race-relations-address-delivered-st-louis-freedom-rally
(accessed 30 January 2023).

Chapter 3

1 The equivalent phrase in the UK is 'a spanner in the works'!
2 Romans 12:2.
3 This is a widely used aphorism, sometimes attributed to Aristotle. Frederick Buechner developed it in his book *Wishful Thinking: A seeker's ABC* (San Francisco, CA: HarperSanFrancisco, 1993), saying: 'the kind of work God usually calls you to is the kind of work (a) that you need most to do and (b) that the world most needs to have done . . . The place God calls you to is the place where your deep gladness and the world's deep hunger meet' (pp. 118–19).
4 These materials are informed by Tony Stolzfus's book *Coaching Questions: A coach's guide to powerful asking skills* (self-published, 2008) and Dawn Barclay's short publication *The Core Values Workbook*, available from her website Living Moxie: https://dawnbarclay.com/core-values.
5 You can hear more about Jan and his story in the 'New Social Enterprises: Starting something new' episode of the *Hopeful Activists* podcast, released on 27 November 2020.
6 As a family, we've even had a go at identifying our shared values, and there's one that probably rings true for a few other families. We put it like this: 'In our family, we like things to be fair.' This is certainly a value that is as fervently held by Nathaniel (aged 4) and Aidan (aged 7)

as it is by Sophie and me. It emerges all the time – from Nathaniel once starting a spontaneous protest on a walk (when he felt strongly that it was unfair for people to shoot pheasants) to arguments about the number of marshmallows each of us has eaten with our hot chocolate!

7 Charlie Mackesy, *The Boy, the Mole, the Fox and the Horse* (London: Ebury Press, 2019) – though the concept of wanting to grow up kind might be older than that!

8 See 'Defining Strengths', Marcus Buckingham, 29 January 2020: www.marcusbuckingham.com/defining-strengths (accessed 4 August 2023).

9 For more on this, see David Comer Kidd and Emanuele Costelo, 'Reading Literary Fiction Improves Theory of Mind', *Science*, vol. 342, no. 6156 (2013), pp. 337–80: https://www.science.org/doi/10.1126/science.1239918 (accessed 30 January 2023).

10 Romans 12:2.

Chapter 4

1 Hebrews 6:19.

2 Hebrews 11:1 KJV.

3 Rubem A. Alves, *Tomorrow's Child: Imagination, creativity and the rebirth of culture* (New York, NY: Harper & Row, 1972), p. 195.

4 Ezekiel 37:1–11.

Chapter 5

1 Find out more about the Snowdrop Project at www.snowdropproject.co.uk.

2 This is a concept used in psychotherapy and was initially developed by Stephen Karpman.

3 For more on this, see Jayakumar Christian, *God of the Empty-Handed: Poverty, power and the kingdom of God* (Uxbridge: World Vision International, 1999) and Bryant L. Myers, *Walking with the Poor: Principles and practices of transformational development*, rev. edn (Maryknoll, NY: Orbis, 2011).

4 Richard Powers, *The Overstory* (New York, NY: W. W. Norton, 2018).

5 See Rosie Kinchen, 'Greta Thunberg on Turning 18 and Why She Won't Tell You Off for Flying', *The Sunday Times*, 2 January 2021: www.thetimes.co.uk/article/greta-thunberg-18-flying-interview-zpf9v0x25 (accessed 30 January 2023) and Caitlin Moran, 'Being Greta Thunberg, the World's Most Extraordinary Teenager', *The Times*, 14 October 2022: www.thetimes.co.uk/article/being-greta-thunberg-the-world-s-most-extraordinary-teenager-caitlin-moran-l6fhqqpl6 (accessed 30 January 2023).

6 1 Corinthians 13:4–6.

Chapter 6

1 Esther 4:16.

2 Kirsty McNeill, 'The Questions Campaigners Hate to Answer, but Need To', Bond, 31 January 2019: www.bond.org.uk/news/2019/01/question-campaigners-hate-to-answer (accessed 30 January 2023).

3 You can hear these stories in the 'Campaign Successes: Starting something new' episode of the *Hopeful Activists* podcast, released on 18 November 2020.

4 A summit of the leaders of Canada, France, Germany, Italy, Japan, the United Kingdom and the United States, seven countries that account for around 50% of global net wealth. In June 2021, the G7 Summit was held in St Ives, Cornwall.

5 A crucial set of climate negotiations, held in Glasgow in November 2021. Around 120 world leaders, along with 40,000 participants, attended; discussions centred on how to keep global warming to 1.5 degrees Celsius.

6 For a more detailed exploration of these reasons, see again Kirsty McNeill's article 'The Question Campaigners Hate to Answer, but Need To': www.bond.org.uk/news/2019/01/question-campaigners-hate-to-answer (accessed 30 January 2023).

7 You can read more about this incredible story here: Gavin Engelbrecht, 'Government Rejects Opencast Mine Proposed by Banks Mining at Druridge Bay', *The Northern Echo*, 8 September 2020: www.thenorthernecho.co.uk/news/18706477.government-rejects-opencast-mine-proposed-banks-mining-druridge-bay (accessed 1 November 2023).

Chapter 7

1 You can hear the full story on the 'Snowdrop: Wisdom for the road' episodes (parts 1 and 2) of the *Hopeful Activists* podcast, released on 20 and 27 September 2019.

2 You can hear the full story on the 'Street Angels: Action in the wild west of Yorkshire' episode of the *Hopeful Activists* podcast, released on 2 May 2019.

3 We don't cover fundraising in any detail because the

specific sources of funding (churches, local authorities, trust funds and so on) vary from area to area and change frequently, but there is lots of information online about this. We've provided some links at the end of this chapter.

4 An alliance of people and organisations using community organising to bring change across the UK. See Citizens UK: citizensuk.org.

5 You can hear this performed on the *Hopeful Activists* podcast in the episode 'The Worship One', released 16 September 2022. Katie's spoken word starts at about thirty-four minutes.

Chapter 8

1 Proverbs 27:17.

Chapter 9

1 Charlie Mackesy, *The Boy, the Mole, the Fox and the Horse* (London: Ebury Press).

2 Luke 10:27 MSG.

3 1 Corinthians 13:2–3.

4 Mackesy, *The Boy, the Mole, the Fox and the Horse* (our italics).

5 1 Peter 4:13.

6 See Romans 12:1.

7 John 10:10.

8 See Matthew 16:24.

9 Lisa Sharon Harper, *The Very Good Gospel: How everything wrong can be made right* (New York, NY: WaterBrook, 2016), p. 41.

10 Psalm 1:3.

11 John 15:5.

12 Romans 7:15.

13 Brené Brown, 'FOR ACC Boundaries, Empathy, and Compassion', YouTube, uploaded by G. Davis, 30 April 2017: https://youtu.be/xATF5uYVRkM (accessed 20 January 2023).

14 Edwin Arrison on the *Hopeful Activists* podcast: 'Lessons from 100 Christian Activists', 29 July 2022.

15 Jo Musker-Sherwood on the *Hopeful Activists* podcast: 'How to Stay Well When the World Is Burning', 9 July 2021. Read more about Jo's work at Climate Emergence: www.climateemergence.co.uk.

Chapter 10

1 You can hear more from Jen on the 2022 Christmas special of the *Hopeful Activists* podcast: 'God With Us', released on 16 December 2022.

Bibliography

Alves, Rubem A. *Tomorrow's Child: Imagination, creativity and the rebirth of culture* (New York, NY: Harper & Row, 1972).

Bailey, Kenneth E. *Jesus through Middle Eastern Eyes: Cultural studies in the Gospels* (Downers Grove, IL: InterVarsity Press, 2008).

Boom, Corrie Ten, with John and Elizabeth Sherrill. *The Hiding Place* (London: Hodder & Stoughton, 2004).

Brown, Brené. 'FOR ACC Boundaries, Empathy, and Compassion', YouTube, uploaded by G. Davis, 30 April 2017: www.youtube.com/watch?v=xATF5uYVRkM.

Buckingham, Marcus. 'Defining Strengths', Marcus Buckingham, 29 January 2020: www.marcusbuckingham. com/defining-strengths (accessed 4 August 2023).

Buechner, Frederick. *Wishful Thinking: A seeker's ABC* (San Francisco, CA: HarperSanFrancisco, 1993).

Christian, Jayakumar. *God of the Empty-Handed: Poverty, power and the kingdom of God* (Uxbridge: World Vision International, 1999).

Engelbrecht, Gavin. 'Government Rejects Opencast Mine Proposed by Banks Mining at Druridge Bay', *The Northern Echo*, 8 September 2020: www.thenorthernecho. co.uk/news/18706477.government-rejects-opencast-mine-proposed-banks-mining-druridge-bay (accessed 30 January 2023).

Gower, Rich, and Abigail Thomas. 'Street Angels: Action in

the wild west of Yorkshire', *Hopeful Activists* podcast, Praxis Centre for Hope and Activism, 2 May 2019.

——. 'Snowdrop Part 1: Wisdom for the road: Lara Bundock and Rachel Medina', *Hopeful Activists* podcast, Praxis Centre for Hope and Activism, 20 September 2019.

——. 'Snowdrop Part 2: Wisdom for the road: Lara Bundock and Rachel Medina', *Hopeful Activists* podcast, Praxis Centre for Hope and Activism, 27 September 2019.

——. 'Campaign Successes: Starting something new', *Hopeful Activists* podcast, Praxis Centre for Hope and Activism, 18 November 2020.

——. 'New Social Enterprises: Starting something new', *Hopeful Activists* podcast, 27 November 2020.

——. 'How to Stay Well When the World Is Burning', *Hopeful Activists* podcast, Praxis Centre for Hope and Activism, 9 July 2021.

——. 'Lessons from 100 Christian Activists', *Hopeful Activists* podcast, Praxis Centre for Hope and Activism, 29 July 2022.

——. 'The Worship One', *Hopeful Activists* podcast, Praxis Centre for Hope and Activism, 16 September 2022.

——. 'God With Us: Christmas special 2022', *Hopeful Activists* podcast, Praxis Centre for Hope and Activism, 16 December 2022.

Harper, Lisa Sharon. *The Very Good Gospel: How everything wrong can be made right* (New York, NY: WaterBrook, 2016).

Kandiah, Krish, with Miriam Kandiah. *Home for Good: Making a difference for vulnerable children* (London: Hodder & Stoughton, 2013).

Kidd, David Comer, and Emanuele Costelo. 'Reading Literary Fiction Improves Theory of Mind', *Science*, vol. 342, no. 6156 (2013), pp. 337–80: www.science.org/doi/10.1126/science.1239918 (accessed 30 January 2023).

Kinchen, Rosie. 'Greta Thunberg on Turning 18 and Why She Won't Tell You Off for Flying', *The Sunday Times*, 2 January 2021: www.thetimes.co.uk/article/greta-thunberg-18-flying-interview-zpf9v0x25 (accessed 30 January 2023).

King Jr, Martin Luther. 'A Realistic Look at the Question of Progress in the Area of Race Relations', address delivered at St Louis freedom rally, 10 April 1957, The Martin Luther King, Jr. Research and Education Institute, Stanford University: kinginstitute.stanford.edu/king-papers/realistic-look-question-progress-area-race-relations-address-delivered-st-louis-freedom-rally (accessed 30 January 2023).

Lewis, C. S. *The Last Battle* (London: Diamond, 1999).

Mackesy, Charlie. *The Boy, the Mole, the Fox and the Horse* (London: Ebury Press, 2019).

McNeill, Kirsty. 'The Question Campaigners Hate to Answer, but Need To', Bond, 31 January 2019: www.bond.org.uk/news/2019/01/question-campaigners-hate-to-answer (accessed 30 January 2023).

Moran, Caitlin. 'Being Greta Thunberg, the World's Most Extraordinary Teenager', *The Times*, 14 October 2022: www.thetimes.co.uk/article/being-greta-thunberg-the-world-s-most-extraordinary-teenager-caitlin-moran-l6fhqqpl6 (accessed 30 January 2023).

Musker-Sherwood, Jo. Climate Emergence: www.climateemergence.co.uk (accessed 31 January 2023).

Myers, Bryant L. *Walking with the Poor: Principles and practices of transformational development*, rev. edn (Maryknoll, NY: Orbis, 2011).

Northumbria Community. 'How Then Shall We Live?': www.northumbriacommunity.org/articles (accessed 31 January 2023).

Powers, Richard. *The Overstory* (New York, NY: W. W. Norton, 2018).

Rilke, Rainer Maria. *Letters to a Young Poet*, trans. Charlie Louth (London: Penguin, 2011).

'Shalom – Peace'. YouTube, uploaded by BibleProject, 30 November 2017: www.youtube.com/watch?v=oLYORLZOaZE.

Wright, N. T. *Surprised by Hope: Rethinking heaven, the resurrection, and the mission of the Church* (London: SPCK, 2008).